I0628412

Our Dance
WITH WORDS

A Collection
of Fine Writing
from
Northern California
Authors

Pretty Road Press
FOLSOM CALIFORNIA

Our Dance with Words:
A Collection of Fine Writing from Northern California Authors

Published by
Pretty Road Press
P.O. Box 273
Folsom, California 95763
www.PrettyRoadPress.com

This book is independently published by Pretty Road Press in arrangement with individual members of Northern California Publishers & Authors.

www.NorCalPA.org

© 2016. All editorial contributions and biographies are copyrighted individually by each respective author. All contributing authors have granted a license to Pretty Road Press to allow for inclusion of their work in this book.

© 2016, Pretty Road Press as to cover, form, and design. All rights reserved.

Cover Design and Photography by Ted Witt
Dance Photo © Elkor, iStockphoto by Getty Images
Ballet Dancer © Andrey Bandurenko by Fotolia.com

Printed in the United States of America

ISBN 978-0-9964910-4-4

20 19 18 17 16   5 4 3 2 1

Contents

Introduction

Thank you for your support of Northern California writers in the purchase of this book. The stories inside this volume are bound to help you find that ah-ha moment. You are also likely to enjoy a laugh or shed a tear.

As president of the Northern California Publishers and Authors, I asked Northern California's finest writers to contribute to this anthology. They responded with enthusiasm, combining original ideas with their unique writing styles. Their work truly is a dance with words. As you read each page, you'll conclude these are stories that beg to be told.

These writers represent just a sample of the undiscovered talent that resides throughout the northern reaches of the Golden State. We appreciate your readership and hope you are rewarded with the discovery of a new and favorite author.

Now, find your favorite beverage. Pull out your favorite snack and spend some quality time enjoying the talents inside.

Dennis L. Potter
President, 2014-15
Northern California Publishers & Authors

Frances Kakugawa

Frances H. Kakugawa, an award-winning author and poet who lives in Sacramento, was born and raised on the Big Island of Hawaii in Kapoho, which was demolished by lava when she was 18. She taught in Michigan, Hawaii, and Micronesia and served as a teacher, trainer, curriculum writer, and lecturer for the University of Hawaii.

In 2002, she was recognized in *Living Legacy: Outstanding Women of the 20th Century in Hawaii.*

Her children's books and her *Kapoho: Memoir of a Modern Pompeii* have received awards from the Hawaii Publishers Award for Excellence and from Northern California Publishers & Authors. Today, she continues to write and conducts poetry writing support groups for caregivers. She also leads writing workshops for adults and children, and lectures on caregiving and poetry throughout the United States.

Visit her website at www.FrancesK.org or read her blog at FrancesKakugawa.WordPress.com. Also connect at Facebook.com//FrancesKakugawa.

FRANCES KAKUGAWA
The Unfinished Dance

We should not have started the dance. But we did. He was the one with pain in his eyes.

There was nothing I couldn't do that weekend. Published twice with books of poetry, I had given myself a writer's weekend on Molokai. I planned to live like a writer, out of my cultural webs, free and daring. I walked into the hotel with my portable typewriter and a thin collection of poetry I planned to build into a full manuscript. Before I could even unpack, "She's a writer" buzzed around the hotel. "Your typewriter," one of the maids explained. "Only writers come here with typewriters."

I spent the first evening at the poolside with my antennae fully extended, hoping to find a poem or two from the cool summer evening. The ink was flowing; the pool was surrounded by men on R & R from Vietnam. The moon was full, and soft chatter filled the air.

The Molokai Trio, with ukuleles in hand, approached me. "Come dance *Yellow Ginger Lei* again."

Scotch and water over ice had started the first dance an hour earlier in the dining room. The Trio moved table to table, serenading diners with Hawai'ian melodies. I sipped scotch and water over ice. They reached my table and asked if I had a request.

"Do you know *Yellow Ginger Lei?*"

They sang the first line in harmony. I boldly asked, "Can I dance?" I took the outstretched hand—I'll blame it on the scotch—stood and danced the hula while they sang and strummed. We stopped diners' forks in mid-air, a tourist's delight.

"Dance another one," they said.

I whispered sheepishly, "I only know *Yellow Ginger Lei.*"

Beside the pool now, they didn't need to ask twice. With the lingering effects of scotch and a half-written poem bolstering my courage, we became the Molokai Foursome. I danced around the pool under romantic Tiki flares flickering shadows upon us. The men on R & R applauded, appearing to be happy with drinks and song. Except for one. He was the one with pain in his eyes.

"You're the writer," he later said.

"Yes," I answered. "Tell me about Vietnam." I shouldn't have listened.

A helicopter pilot, he had one mission, always the same: to fly down and search for children survivors among the villagers who lay dying or dead beneath our American bombs. Each flight had room for only a few children. Forced to play God, he walked among the dead and wounded, selecting the children who seemed the most alive for another chance at life. Did he hear a whimper? Did that child move? He gathered what life he could find and flew the broken bodies back to the field hospital…mission never accomplished.

He preserved what he saw with what he did with his brush and oil paints. He painted the children as wooden logs, splattered red, on canvas after canvas, his own despair hidden beneath each deliberate brush stroke. No words were yet invented for what he felt.

A week before R & R and after many more missions, he looked for his canvases and paint, only to find them being tossed into a bonfire by his superiors. "You can't take these home; the war stays here." The wooden logs burned to ash, but the scent would follow him home and cling on for the rest of his life.

It was a story for poets.

Three days later, his stories continued over cups of tea in my studio apartment in Honolulu. He told his stories, his hand grasped around my blue and white teacup, like those children clinging to life. The aroma of green tea failed to diffuse the agony in his voice. I put my hand over his. We would never be the same.

His body shook, going off the Richter scale. I was young, a Zelda, a Sylvia, a poet, believing I could help conquer anything with poetry and love if he stayed. But he was wiser. He would write in his journal later:

I was drawn to her soft voice, her eager searching words.

She drew me out of my defensive shell. I told her of the boring hours interspersed with moments of terror. The words didn't come easily; the memories were still too fresh in my mind, but I found myself unable to stop, and with each word I became more depressed, more agitated. I told her of the Navy Seals, how they made jokes about the body parts. She let me go on, her eyes never leaving my face. My hurt became her hurt. I could not stop. I'd found someone to help me release the demons in myself.

I wanted to stay and never leave. What a quandary I found myself in.

I knew this demon in me would cause her great harm.

"Stay," I wanted to say, but like steam from our tea cups, I let it dissipate into silence.

He returned to his home in Virginia, promising he'd be back. He wrote with sharpened pencils, each word etched on paper, with caution and passion. He called me Darling. I was the brilliant, powerful, femme fatale poet.

I replied with fountain pens wet with ink, becoming Elizabeth Barrett Browning, Emily Dickinson, Sylvia Plath. I wrote him a poem, *The Wooden Soldier*, believing poetry was stronger than wartime memories.

The Wooden Soldier

The wooden soldier marches
As he was wound to do.
Steadily, rhythmically,
Mechanical precision.

The only dislocation
Between manufactured knees.
The wooden soldier marches
Then stands perfectly still,
A soldier no more
But a wooden peg.

But the soldier I know
Keeps on marching.
He keeps on beating

For he has no key
To stop him from seeing
Dislocated limbs
Of children on children.

He has no key
To stop him from smelling
The river of blood
On Sunday afternoons.

Forgive us, O Soldier
For factorizing keys
Only for soldiers
On wooden knees.

Forgive us, soldier
For mechanized birds,
Wooden logs and battlefields.

It was a time for love, for poetry that begged to be written, rapidly, endlessly, before the last verse was finished. He sketched a wooden soldier holding a small injured child—to be painted someday.

Then, like the sharp cracking sound of lightning, shattering windows, like a giant wave knocking me over, filling my lungs with the sea, his letter arrived:

Do not write anymore. This is it. It's all over.
Forgive me; it's all over. Do not write.

I disobeyed. I wrote and wrote, poem after poem, but I never sent them. They, with *Wooden Soldier,* were read by everyone else nine months later in my third book of poetry, *Golden Spike.*

Defiantly determined to have the last word, I included one of his poems. I dedicated the book to "Someone I Know" and sent him a copy.

The unpublished poems, I saved in a shoe box, labeled "Private:" penetrating arrows, razor sharp, tearing through cardboard, bleeding red; poetry, destructive as warplanes over villages. Red ink dripped from the tip of my pen, long after the last word was written. As time would have it, the red faded, and the shoe box remained an attic for old memories.

Thirty-three years later, a letter arrived from New York, forwarded by my publisher. I recognized the penciled words.

I wandered into Borders in Syracuse. I must tell you, you've never, never been far from my thoughts. I was poking through the poetry area, always wondering if, hoping you might have published another book after Golden Spike. *Much to my delight, like a punch in the stomach, there was your* Mosaic Moon. *I debated for weeks, should I? Why not?*

I'm sorry, but I had to let you go because I was going down and couldn't take you with me. I returned from Vietnam, damaged, one of the forgotten men. PTSD was not invented yet, so all the help I got were shrugs and sleeping drugs. Helpless, I had nowhere to turn so I saved all my drugs, and at that very moment of ending my life, I heard your voice, intruding into my thought... In spite of my anger—my effort to push you aside to seek the comfort of nothingness— your voice became louder and louder. I believe it was my love for you. I have no other words for what pulled me back from the brink of self-destruction.

I would have destroyed you. It was the hardest thing I ever had to do when I ended it. I was having frightening dreams, ducked at sudden sounds. I stayed awake to prevent the dreams. I slept with women to ease the memories; almost caused the death of one. A helicopter was receiving hostile fire. I was going into a hot landing, and the damned thing refused to respond to UP Collective. The landing was rough. The bird began to roll over. I leaped out of bed, shouting and screaming, pulling a crew member out of the burning chopper. I woke up with my hands around the throat of a woman in bed with me. I had to let you go to protect you.

I still have dreams, but they live in the shadows now. The instinctive ducking at loud noises come less and less. Molokai is alive as ever.

Still too poetically naive, still Sylvia and Zelda, I wrote, "I would have glued all the pieces together." I wasn't young anymore, and he was still, wiser.

A few phone calls and emails later, once again, like circling vultures waiting for death, the old message echoed through cyberspace.

> *I'm sorry. Don't get in touch anymore.*
> *Until I lay Molokai and Vietnam to rest, I need peace, peace without you.*
> *This is hard to write—am angry with you for patiently letting me open up the war, coming to terms to what I need to do. Damn you. I can no longer accept shrugs and sleeping drugs from the VA. I need an overhaul of myself, and I need to do this without you.*

His penciled words have faded once again. "Someday," he had said, before departing, "write our story." This, I could do.

To be continued.

Golden Spike

The signs were there: when students need to talk
they hang around my desk, playing with my stapler or
realigning my pens and pencils until there is privacy
for courage to emerge.

"Sometimes," she quietly started, still playing with pencils,
"I get up at three in the morning and hear my dad crying.
I go downstairs, and he's sitting on steps, crying in the dark.
He was in the Vietnam War; he won't talk about it,
but I watch him cry a lot. He can't sleep. I know because I always
see him on the steps. I wish I knew how to help him."

Damn! Here's that war again.
No child ought to be wakened at 3:00 a.m. by a father's tears.
No child ought to be sucked in, to twenty-five-year-old wars.
No child ought to have dreams of brightly crayoned images
disrupted by black ashes.

I wasn't trained to undo the nature of war.
I didn't know how to banish the phantoms of war.
Maybe...maybe...I gave her a copy of Golden Spike.

"I wrote these poems about the war.
Maybe your dad will find this book helpful."

A few weeks later, I read in her class journal: Private to Miss K:
My dad is always reading your book.
He carries it around with him, and he's not getting up anymore,
he's not crying anymore. Thank you for helping him.
Is it okay if I keep the book a bit longer? He wants to know,
did you know someone from the Vietnam War?

"Yes," I wrote in her journal,
"Tell your dad I knew someone just like him."

On the last day of school, once again she stood near my desk.
"I'm sorry I haven't returned your book, but my dad
is still reading your book. I hate to take the book away from him."
"I gave that book to both of you. I'm so glad
my poems help him."

She held on to our hug, whispering,
"Thank you, Miss Kakugawa."

Dennis Potter

Dennis Potter is the immediate past president of Northern California Publishers & Authors. As president of the organization, he had the vision for this anthology and issued the call to some of Northern California's best writers to submit the stories, essays, and poetry that have now led to *Our Dance with Words*.

A engineer by trade, he exercises his right-brain talents as the creator of the character Jake Burns, whom Potter describes as the uncommon, common man. Through all his lives, Jake Burns attacks life with enthusiasm, determination, and humor. He is equally at home eating a hot dog from a street vendor or attending a ballet.

Potter and his family live in Lincoln, California. Communicate with him at DennisPotter56@ aol.com.

DENNIS POTTER
Maiko and Jake

Maiko and I may have grown old together, but our love has never grown old. We have been blessed with children, grandchildren, and great-grandchildren. Maiko's health has deteriorated. She now uses a walker or a wheelchair—a hard transition for a dancer. She spent her life teaching dance, as a professional ballet soloist, and directing a ballet company. In her heart and mind, she remains a dancer. Several times I have seen her sitting in a chair with her eyes shut and a smile on her lips. In those moments, I know she is dancing again.

Two years ago my chest started to feel frail as if it were constructed of fine glass. A few months later, my heart would occasionally skip a few beats. Lately, it performs its own dance—what I describe as a slow roll, a heartbeat that takes two seconds to complete. It leaves me breathless.

This morning, moments before I got out of bed, I was greeted with a double roll. My body felt like an old ship starting to break up. With the speed of an arthritic sloth, I climbed out of bed. I didn't want to wake Maiko. I'm old, and the double roll sapped a lot of energy.

I struggled through my morning routine in the bathroom. The mirror's reflection reminded me how old I am. I stuck my tongue out at the old man looking at me; he returned the favor. I shuffled my way to the kitchen to make breakfast for the both of us.

When Maiko started to have major problems with her hips and legs, we had this new house built. Our old house stood three stories with a full basement. This house sits smaller, just one story, making it easier for Maiko to move through. We gave our old house to an orphanage when we moved here. Once in a while, we visit the old house, just to evoke memories and bask in the energy of the children.

Our present house tops an isolated hill, quiet and serene. From our kitchen window, we look out over the city of Nishura. From our garden on the opposite side of the house, we watch the boats and ships floating in Mikara Bay.

When I finished setting up a light breakfast, I returned to the bedroom. Maiko was still sleeping, so I eased myself into a rocking chair next to our bed. As I sat, I felt my heart flutter. I closed my eyes and felt my strength slowly ebbing. I could feel each and every broken bone and every strained ligament that I had ever suffered. I heard Maiko stir.

I opened my eyes and said, "Good morning, dear."

Maiko smiled, "Good morning, Jake."

"How are you?"

"I feel tired, very tired."

"Let's get you up, and we will have breakfast."

"I don't feel hungry."

"Just a little breakfast?"

I assisted Maiko to the bathroom and helped her through her morning regimen. Finally, I helped her dress, and then I brushed her beautiful, silky, snow-white hair. Using a walker, she casually strolled to the kitchen alongside me. I assisted Maiko into her chair. She had a hand on my chest as my heart choreographed another roll; Maiko detected it through her palm.

"Jake, what just happened!"

My ship was taking on water. I took a deep breath and said, "I think old age and my misspent youth are catching up with me."

As we ate, Maiko exclaimed, "I feel so very weak! I'm afraid, Jake."

I reached out and held her hand. "Don't be afraid. Everything will be just fine. Soon you will be dancing again."

"I'm dying," she said.

"We're dying."

"Will you please hold me?"

"I'll do better than that."

I stood and helped Maiko into her wheelchair. I expended most of my remaining strength pushing Maiko out to our garden and then helping her sit on a bench. I kicked the wheelchair away and sat beside my wife. Now the water was nearly up to my ship's railing. Maiko leaned against me. I put an arm around her and drew her to me. We looked out over the bay. The bay was calm and the sunshine reflected off the water like diamonds. The sailboats shined bright with color.

"What happens now?" she asked.

"I think we will fall asleep and wake up in another world."

"Together?"

"That I don't know. I do know that we will be together again. I also know that I will watch you dance again."

Maiko rested her head against my chest. "I remember that first time you watched me dance."

"I'm amazed you remember," I said. "You were so mad at me at the time. The flames in your eyes nearly set the ceiling on fire."

"I was mad because you stole my heart. I looked out at you from inside my studio. My heart was instantly lost to you. You upset my whole world in just one second. One look into your eyes and I was yours." She looked up at me and said, "You still have those same beautiful, deep-blue eyes. You may have gotten older, but you eyes haven't aged one minute."

I gave Maiko a light kiss on her forehead, "You, dear, are just as beautiful as you were when you melted my heart that same day. Even when you were chewing me out, warning me to be on my best behavior, I began to love you. All it took was to watch you dance as you taught that class; I knew that I wasn't going to let you out of my life."

"You younger guys always say the right things."

"Ah yes, but only to older ladies who deserve it."

"Somehow after all these many years two years' difference in our ages doesn't mean a thing."

"It never did."

"Do you know what I have always remembered you doing?"

"No, dear, what is it?" I asked.

"You and that horse Samson flying over the ground. Both of you were magnificent. Samson's tail and mane were flying, and you had that silly grin of yours as you leaned forward over his neck."

"I remember when you did your first performance as a soloist. You were so beautiful, and you communicated your joy of dance to the whole audience. They all danced through you that night."

We fell into a silence. It broke when we simultaneously said, "I love you."

I felt Maiko stiffen. "Dear, just relax."

My chest did another full roll. My ship now floundered, the stern engulfed. Maiko seemed to hold her breath, then she released it with a soft sigh.

I whispered, "Goodbye, Maiko. I love you. I'll see you soon."

Out of my shirt pocket, I pulled up a signaling device given to us by our children. When we moved to this house, our family worried about how isolated it was. If we needed any help, we simply were to push the big, red button; help would come running. If my timing were right, pushing that red button would be the last thing I would do.

I looked out over the bay and relaxed. Maiko had only left me but moments ago. Already I felt so lonely. Old I can take; old without Maiko I cannot. I had a wonderful life, more than seventy years with Maiko. How can I live without her? I wondered what would happen next. Next was my chest dancing a massive double roll. My ship's engine sputtered, stopped. My vessel quickly began to slide under the waves. I pushed the button, dropping the device to the ground. I wrapped my other arm around Maiko, closed my eyes, and followed her.

M.L. Edson

Mary Lou Edson is best known as the author of *The Six Rivers Killer*. Author, poet, and teacher, she was born and raised in California. She taught all ages, from elementary to community college students, before going on to spend twenty years teaching at CSP-Sacamento, New Folsom Prison, and other California correctional facilities.

 *The Six Rivers Killer* is a fictionalized story of an actual murder case that took place in Humboldt County, California. *Not Even a Shadow* is a journal of her time working in the juvenile facility and contrasts young wards to older inmates. She has also written *Grammar Guardian*, a quick grammar and punctuation guide; *Doing Life with a Map*, a workbook co-authored with Lee Bowman, to help young people stay out of prison; and *Poems from an Old White Broad*.

Mary Lou also offers editing and critiquing services as well as grammar and punctuation workshops. She can be contacted at marylouwriter@yahoo.com.

M.L. EDSON
Ghosts

Ghost stories abound with tales of sightings in Old Sacramento. There's even a photograph in our store that a local artist took while touring the Underground, which was created in the 1850s when the buildings in that area were raised about nine feet to avoid devastating floods.

The photo hanging on the back wall contains rocky walls that are now the foundations for the stores above, dirt floors, and a shadow of a cowboy who is apparently dressed in a western duster and a cowboy hat. Smoke rises from the area where his face would be. The shadow of the cowboy and the smoke are there, but no one is standing nearby — there is nothing but the rocks and dirt

Most people discount the ghostly rumors and pictures as hokum, untrue, false. *There's no such thing as ghosts. They're just the result of an over-active imagination.* But Marleen, the photographer, swears it's true. It's a real photograph. She didn't edit the photo. Didn't re-touch it.

I'm in the group of "most people" who don't trust those incidents and reports. *There's no such thing as ghosts.*

You know when we see some movement out of the corner of your eye? Well, that's our imagination. No one is there. No anomaly is passing through the light waves, causing a temporal or visual distortion. It's simply a tear duct pumping extra liquid into our eye socket and diverting our normal vision into a wave, giving the impression that someone, or something, is there.

Every one of these incidents can be explained away, right? Right.

However, while working in our store in Old Sacramento last Tuesday morning, I recalled an incident from my youth that made me think again about the possibility of ghosts.

When I was about ten years old, I wasn't feeling well and stayed home from school. In those days it was safe for a child to stay home alone. It was also a time when our pets could roam the neighborhood without being fenced in or constantly on a leash. Our dog Riley was outside.

So, there I was—alone in the house. Still in PJs and wrapped in my terrycloth bathrobe, I snuggled on the living room couch wishing we had that new device that some friends already had—a television. I had nothing to do but read, so I sat with a book in my lap.

Suddenly, the front door opened slightly. I sat up expecting my mom or dad to enter coming home from work to check on me. No. The door slowly opened, and Riley walked in, glanced at me, and continued through the living room and into the dining room.

I got up, closed the door, and followed the dog. We had a multi-purpose kitchen—an eat-in table tucked into a cubby and a washer and dryer near the back door leading to the carport and back yard.

I stopped short halfway into the kitchen. Riley had walked past the dryer, and it turned on. No one, and no part of the dog, had touched the dryer. It switched on all by itself.

Tingles ran down my back, and goosebumps appeared on my arms when the next thing happened. In fact, goose bumps still tickle my arms whenever I think about it. The back door opened. Opened in. No one was outside pushing on it. Riley didn't bite the doorknob and turn it. He didn't stick his nose into a door that was partially opened. It wasn't. It had been firmly closed. The door simply opened by itself as the dog approached, and he walked right out to the backyard

I later wrote about this incident for a junior high assignment and only received a *C* grade for my effort. *"Too fantastic. Obviously made up. Couldn't have happened,"* the teacher had said as he firmly planted the average grade on the paper. *"You can't believe this really happened. Don't be silly."*

I don't believe in ghosts. Honestly, I don't. Denial worked for me for decades.

Then today.

Ghosts don't exist. They can't.

The store in Old Sacramento had been open for half an hour, and still no customers had come in. A storm had stalled after a downpour earlier this morning, and gray clouds hung over the old buildings and cobbled streets. No one was walking on the boardwalks; no one was shopping even though it was now dry. I was busy dusting displays in the back of the store.

Ghosts aren't possible. They can't be.

Christmas music played softly over the speakers, and it was otherwise quiet in the store

Tinkling glass.

I turned. Still no one was in the store. I returned to dusting the trinkets and artwork.

Breaking glass.

I spun around and headed toward the front door where Christmas ornaments hung on an artificial tree. Approaching the front area, slightly obscured behind a three-foot display and shelves, I searched the floor. *An ornament must have dropped to the wood planks and shattered.*

Nothing.

Confused, I looked around and under the shelves.

Nothing.

I searched outside the open, front door. Maybe someone had dropped something just outside.

Nothing. Still nothing.

I shrugged and returned to my chores.

Within ten minutes, I heard shattering glass once again. This time I was so certain that something had fallen and broken that I stopped in the office that was mid-way through the store. I grabbed the broom and dustpan. Once again I searched the floor and shelves at the front.

Nothing. There's no way that ghosts can exist.

Everything was in order.

A couple came in and found me standing there holding the broom and dustpan with a confused look on my face, so I hurriedly returned the items to their places in the office before helping them with their purchases.

Since nothing was amiss, I continued to work the store the

rest of the day. There were a few light showers during the day, many customers, several buyers, but no further incidents until fifteen minutes before closing time. My next chore was to count the cash in the drawer, tally up the sales, and balance the accounting from the charges.

A customer came in and stopped just inside the front door.

"Good evening," I said to the older gentleman. "Welcome."

"Hello, young lady," he answered. He was dressed in clothes out of fashion for decades. He wore a broad-brimmed hat and a dusty overcoat, a bit odd for the wet weather we'd been having. He cleared his throat and stepped toward the Christmas display where many ornaments and decorations hung. "Did you know you have a couple of broken ornaments up here?"

"What? No? You're kidding." Shivers once again ran up my spine and down my arms. "Let me see." I rushed from behind the counter to the store front.

A faint odor of bitter cigarette smoke permeated the air around the gentleman as he shuffled past me farther into the store. "Nice things in here. Pretty."

"Thank you," I said as I hurried to the office to get the broom and dustpan. I passed him on my way back to sweep up the mess. The cigarette odor hung heavy. "I'll be right with you," I told him.

"Take your time. I'm in no hurry."

I swooped up the broken glass ornaments and headed to the back of the counter to dump the pieces into the wastebasket then returned the broom and dustpan to the office. The gentleman was at the rear of the store, just beyond the office as I entered to re-hang the items on their hooks near the door. It took all of two seconds

"Let me know if you need any help," I said as I exited the office and turned toward the back area.

Empty.

Odd.

No one had passed by the office door while I was in there.

No footsteps were heard.

A faint odor of pungent cigarette smoke lingered as I searched the store for him, even checking the sidewalk outside the storefront.

Empty. No one was there. No one.

I was nearly ready to look under the counters when I glanced at the wall where the photographs hung. The one of the ghost in the Underground Passages of Old Sacramento was lopsided

As I reached up to straighten it, I will still swear the shadow winked at me.

Then I noticed something different in the picture. There was a shadow of a dog standing near his feet.

I had never noticed that before

Kimberly A. Edwards

K imberly A. Edwards writes articles, memoir, and creative non-fiction.
   Her work has appeared in national and international media. A member of the American Society of Journalists and Authors and International Food Wine and Travel Association, she has held officer positions in the California Writers Club, where she received the 2013 Jack London Award for service.

She has been the publisher of a monthly 12-page newsletter for writers that covered national trends, markets, and industry leaders.

Currently she is coordinating the NCPA Student Scholarship Program. She also leads a Memories…Memoir Seminar through the California State University, Sacramento Renaissance Society.

KIMBERLY A. EDWARDS
Stumped by the Grump

Several years ago, I lived in a house in Carmichael, California, backing up to the American River Parkway, a buffer of canopied oak, cottonwoods, wild fennel and mustard, deer, rabbits, hawks, and blackberry vines. Since the arms of nature were known to claim visitors, we kept our pets close to home. It was here that my daughter brought a cat home from the SPCA. His black fur contrasted with his white spots like day and night, tame and wild, truth and lie.

There was also a disparity in his disposition. One minute he'd be silent, the next, cranky. Spook, as we came to call him, transversed the scale from mute to frenzy with little warning. He started with curious moans, low throaty complaints pelted in intervals, picking up speed, building to bursts belted out like bullets at the pace of a sheep's bleat. Anguish flooded these outbursts. There seemed to be no way of predicting the events that unleashed them.

Meanwhile, my daughter Elaine, age 11, was entering a touchy phase. The signs were clear, as nothing was ever right with her: hair, homework, or curfew. I increased her allowance, took her shopping, and extended her privileges. As her mother, I thought I knew what she wanted, but I didn't.

As Spook's new family, we tried inducements to please him: treats, toys, scratching posts, petting and cooing, which sent his ears flicking back and forth. We fed him chicken nibbles, gave him access to the backyard, and padded a basket for private naps. Nothing seemed to temper his moods.

One morning as the sun rose over the river and streamed into the room that faced the backyard, Elaine tested Spook's mysterious malaise. Picking him up in the course of his whimper, she mimicked his pitch. He countered with a yelp. Drawing him close, she howled. He broke into a wail. A glaze swept over his eyes as if drawing on some far-off memory. Together he and Elaine yowled like coyote siblings on a moonlit trail. From that day forward, whenever Spook launched his woe, Elaine engaged him in concert—two sets of chords meshed into one united lamentation.

As the duo performed, the scent of licorice from wild fennel wafted from the riverbank behind the house. The feline's head bobbed up and down, wedge-shaped jaw flapping madly, all the while crooning staccato amid the scent of native spices. Never in two years did I decipher a particular tune, only a mournful call, filled with desire for something just beyond the back door.

Each afternoon, as the sun came around to the front of the house, a luxury sports car passed, the driver always wearing a scowl. He did not wave back. He gunned the engine in front of my home, discharging exhaust. I told Elaine, "That man must not have any friends. You have to be nice to have a friend."

One late fall day, Spook lost his collar. I delayed in buying him another. Meanwhile, new school friendships consumed Elaine. When she was home, she buried her face in the phone. I adopted two kittens.

Time and again Spook climbed the back fence. I must admit, I didn't try to stop him; anyway, he resisted being held.

Rain came; the river rose. Spook's absences grew. Elaine was distracted by friends. I felt annoyed. Why did the cat disappear for days, leaving me worried, when we gave him everything? I told myself, "He'll be back, as this is his home."

But finally, when he was gone for a week and didn't return, I began to speculate about the area behind us, where coyotes sometimes roamed. With time I accepted Spook's fate and doted on the kittens, which loved to be cuddled.

Just before spring, we planned to move. On the morning of the big day, Elaine came to me, her face as opaque as the mist that hung over the river. "I just saw Spook in a window down the street," she said.

I couldn't believe such news. Four months had passed since

we'd seen him. "Not likely our Spook," I said. "He wouldn't stay so close without coming home."

"It's Spook," she said, her welling eye lit by a sprig of sun slipping in the screen door.

Her distress caused me to think that as a mother I needed to resolve any concern that Spook dwelled nearby. So while the movers boxed our belongings, I hurried over to the scene of the sighting, a residence down the street.

After ringing the bell, I wondered what I would do if Spook were really there though I knew he wasn't. A deadbolt turned. Who appeared, but the man who drove the lavish cars—he who never waved nor smiled.

A chill swept over the porch. "Afternoon," I said, facing the grouch whose glare was as cold up close as from my window. "We saw a cat—"

"Mittens," he interrupted.

"My daughter's cat Spook—"

"Mittens is our cat," he corrected.

"Perhaps I could see the cat. My daughter—"

"I'll talk to my wife," he grumbled. "She'll be devastated. Come back in two hours."

I faced a range of emotions. How could the man be so arrogant? Why today of all days did a black-and-white cat appear? Why not a month or a week earlier—or never? Was it possible that Spook was alive? Would the man give him up without a fight? Could I take Spook back when we now had two kittens? Why had I not posted flyers when first he disappeared?

As the sun inched over our house, the movers finished loading the back of the moving van. I made the dreaded walk to the man's house not knowing what I was going to do if the cat turned out to be our missing town crier.

"My daughter would like to see the cat," I told the man when he opened the door. Next to me stood Elaine. I could feel her hope for reclaiming the cat.

"My wife's crying her eyes out," he spit, producing the cat, clasped between fists. He thrust it toward us for inspection.

With his chalky-white hands clutching the furry torso, all we could do was stroke the coat.

We ran our fingers between the flattened ears. Was it or wasn't it? This cat didn't wiggle. We whispered Spook's name. Its eyes stayed blank: not a flicker of recognition.

Elaine began to hum. Not a peep from the cat. She cued up a song.

I studied the cat's expression for any sign of awareness.

None.

I surveyed the black-and-white markings, the faraway gaze, the triangular little jaw. In a matter of minutes I became convinced that this was Spook.

But the cat known for vocals stayed hushed for the first time in his life.

With the moving van idling in the distance, I debated whether to fight for the cat or leave him.

Should I?

Shouldn't I?

While there was relief in knowing that Spook was alive, his silence was upsetting. Our new kittens always purred in our presence. Here Spook had the audacity to snub us in favor of this irascible man.

That did it. I announced that we were leaving the cat. Elaine looked at me, her eye beginning to fill. We petted him one last time and turned away.

"That's our Spook," she blurted on our way home. "The stupid man stole him!"

"Spook found another home," I replied, masking my own dejection. I remembered him crooning with Elaine as the scent of fennel breached our back door. Oddly, I felt hurt, rebuffed, insulted upon thinking of Spook defecting to another home. Now that the king of despair had a real reason to pine, he lounged in the very hands that gripped him. How could he prefer that terrible man to us?

"Spook gave us a gift," I rationalized.

"He's our cat," said Elaine, bursting into tears.

"And he let us know that he's alright. How many cats have we lost, never knowing what happened?"

"But he really loved us."

"Then he deserves the best," I lied. "Traveling to the vet in shiny cars."

What I didn't say is that I had secretly cursed Spook for being disloyal and for reappearing on the day we were moving.

"He's a different kind of cat," she said.

"Yes, and we'll have to come visit him," I said. I knew this wouldn't happen. Spook and the man were two of a kind. They belonged together. The feline who whined had gone in search of his own and had found it, not by the river, but down the street.

Nic Butterfield

Nic Butterfield is a Northern Californian currently attending the University of Washington in Seattle where she delves into a wide range of topics ranging from environmental sciences to cultural studies. Nic is interested in exploring different forms of storytelling in order to address relevant social issues.

She writes prose and poetry about the complexities of life, both the mundane and the absurd, often attempting to find harmony between the two. She wrote short stories throughout high school, where she served as president of her school's writing club. The group published three anthologies and now runs three writing-based blogs featuring poetry and short prose using non-binary pronouns.

When not writing or blogging, Nic enjoys reading '80s scifi and playing solitaire.

NIC BUTTERFIELD

I Am Above

Q uickly now. Open the book you've never read and extract the note. Take the pencil from your bedside table.

I am ABOVE. This is the 167th— erase the number—the 168th time I have done this. Please do not be alarmed. I am fine.

Place the note on your pillow and make yourself still. Breathe slower. Stop the pounding of your heart. You really shouldn't worry so much. Save that for the daytime.

Quiet yourself. Soon the sheets will stop rustling and your clothes will, too, and silence will prevail in your bedroom. Wait, listen for the sound of your mother's snoring loud and clear in the next room.

Good. She's asleep.

Ever so quietly put your weight on the floor. You know by now which board creaks. Avoid it. Turn the doorknob carefully and pull it shut again behind you. Pass her door and then tread carefully, *carefully* down along the hall.

Remember, she's a light sleeper. Any little sound will wake her.

It's this rush of excitement that makes it all worth it. It's not dangerous. Of course, you wouldn't do anything dangerous. Never. But it's exciting all the same because you could get caught. You *won't* get caught, but you *could*.

Step lightly through the house, that's it. Almost there. Do not mind the walls that surround you. Do not mind the left that presses against you. Do not mind the right that contains you. Do not mind the ceiling that traps you. Do not mind the darkness behind that pulls you back. Only mind the front; forward motion is the only escape. Almost there.

There's a box in front of the door—a new obstacle. Do not flinch; you've dealt with this before. It's closed; you don't know what's inside. There's only one thing to do: hope it won't make any noise.

Slide your fingers beneath the box. It's empty. Let out the breath you've been holding. Relax. Put the box aside, not too far. If you forget to replace it, the cats can be blamed.

This is the difficult part. Lean your weight on the door. Pull up on the handle and turn the little knob to unlock it. Minimal noise. Good. Very good. Push down on the handle and slide open the door.

Feel the cold night air on your body. Really feel it. Let it pull at you, and let it change you slowly. Close your eyes. You can feel the breath of the sky on your skin. But don't wait too long. She'll feel the draft, even subconsciously, and she'll wake.

Close the door as carefully as you opened it. Don't get excited because you have been thus far successful. Any noise at any moment will make this night a defeat. And that would be a shame, wouldn't it, at attempt number one hundred and sixty-eight, to finally fail?

The door slides closed with as little noise as it ever does. Breathe deeply. Let the air fill your lungs. Feel it prick at the skin on your face. It's even more fun in the winter, isn't it? The air is colder, and you have to fight your desire to curl up and sleep. You have to remind yourself you're not a cold-blooded animal immobilized by lower temperatures. Your body is meant to fight the cold. So fight it.

Turn right. Around the corner of the house is the fence. You're nimble now; you know how to do it. Step up on the pile of bricks. Trust yourself not to fall. That's the trick, really. Of course, you might fall. Of course, you'll *probably* fall; of course, you *should* fall, but you haven't, and you won't because you know you won't. That's the trick.

Pull yourself up onto the fence. Balance yourself. It would be silly to fall now. Steady.

Good.

The roof sits merely a half-foot above the fence. Stand up.

You're steady enough by now. First step lands on the fence; second step reaches over the gutter; third step and you're there.

Look, you can see the stars well from here. Not as well as if you were farther away from the city. But they're there. It's the best time of the year for this. After Christmas, so the lights are all down. And it's almost as if the frost in the air adds to their luminescence as they hang up there in the sky.

Sit and stare. Stare at the lights. Don't be afraid. The night is scary *inside*, where it's dark and only dark. Everything surrounds you, everything you've ever done. You can see it play before your eyes; you can feel it weigh upon your shoulders.

But how can you be afraid up here? Up here the stars are with you. No evil can exist beneath the stars; it's just not possible. It's taken you a long time to realize this, but you know it now.

Listen. It'll come if you wait. You hear it every night, always around midnight. Who knows who else hears it? But *you* can hear it, a low rumble in the distance like thunderstorm racing across the sky.

Thump.

What was that? It seems like it came from the next rooftop over, but how can that be?

"Hey! Are you waiting for the train?"

Calm down. No need to panic. Just find the source of the voice. Look. See. Someone's on the other roof.

Just *calm down.*

"Yes, you. Are you waiting for the train?"

A joke, perhaps?

Say: "What train?"

"Isn't this the station?"

Certainly a joke. You're on a roof, not at a train station. Stop shaking your head like that. You look like an idiot.

"Of course not. It wouldn't drive this low."

That was quite a magnificent leap, wasn't it? Straight from that roof to this one. Regard him. Yes, it's a *him* and young like you, thin and tall like an evening shadow. Eyes that seem to glow. You shouldn't be able to tell the color of a person's eyes at night, but his are definitely blue, a cold, sharp blue like ice. He has a bindle over his shoulder, like a good old-fashioned train-hopper. He wears his grin like a garment.

"You wouldn't happen to know where the station is, would you?"

Say: "What station?"

"The train station. I seem to be lost. I haven't stopped here before. I'll be late for the train if I don't get there soon. Oh, you don't know, do you? Hmm. That old man told me something; I know it...it's just..."

My, what is he going on about? Tell him there's a train station downtown.

"On which rooftop?"

Say: "It isn't on any rooftop. It's on the ground like any other train station."

"Well, I'm not looking for The Any-Other Train, I'm looking for the Nightwind Express."

The Nightwind Express?

"It's a train that shoots straight through the atmosphere, touches down on one rooftop, and then back out into the sky."

There's something wrong with this guy.

"Would you like to see it?"

No, you would not like to see it.

"Well, I've got to go. See you around."

Watch him turn. Watch him carefully. And then—oh! Peculiar. But yes, that seems like a ladder from your roof to the next. It simply *appeared*. Or was it there before?

Ask: "Where did the ladder come from?"

"The, er, the light of the stars magnified by the curvature of the atmosphere, it, er, well, the light causes the material to solidify where normally it's...magic. It's magic."

Stare.

"All right. It's not magic. But it's complicated. Are you coming or not?"

Say: "I'm afraid."

"No, you're not."

That grin hasn't left his face. This is a dream. That's it; it's a dream. You fell asleep on the roof, and now you're dreaming.

Well, go on. If it's a dream, you might as well make it an exciting one.

Step on the ladder. It certainly seems solid. The nimbleness you've acquired in recent months will help you follow swiftly after the starlit stranger. Race after him, quickly now. Don't let him get away. Climb one ladder straight up; slide on a pole straight down. Don't stop to stare at the ladders. They could be made of stardust for all you know. That won't make it any easier to climb them.

Cross over the street on a long bridge. Don't fall. Don't— Hold on! Don't let your fingers slip.

Accept his help. Keep running.

The buildings grow taller; they stretch toward the sky. Don't look down. Oh dear, you are up very high, aren't you? The harsh light of the streetlamps glares at you from below. They tell you to come down. Don't listen to them. Streetlamps know nothing of stars.

Pull yourself up onto the rooftop and regard the stranger again. He shrugs.

"Honestly, I thought it was this one."

Say: "Maybe the tallest building? So it doesn't have to be as close to the ground?"

He snaps his fingers at your tentative remark.

"You're one smart kid."

It seems rather obvious to you, doesn't it? Regardless, follow his ambling path up the building via the intricate pattern of ladders and bridges adorning your otherwise ordinary town.

Oh, look, now we're getting poetic about it. Just follow.

Pull yourself onto another rooftop—oh. You're at the top of it all now. Everything is below you, everything in the world for miles. Watch the world drop away from you. Watch everything fade.

No, no, look *up*. Look above you. Have you ever noticed that sometimes the sky looks like it's arching up, like the point directly above your head is the farthest away? Oh, but have you noticed that sometimes it seems as if you could reach right up and touch the sky, that it arches down and then curves away into a deep blue unknown? Have you ever—

Listen.

It must be midnight now; you can hear the thunder? Though it sounds far away, it seems to shake the stars. But it's louder now, louder than ever before. Turn to the stranger. Ask him what is happening!

He laughs. That's all right; let the smile through. It's a marvelous sight. It's a marvelous sound. It's a marvelous feeling through your bones.

"It's the train!"

His voice seems to be ripped away from the both of you as the sound gets louder, louder, *louder*. There it is.

A moment ago it was a star, but now it's brighter like it's moving toward you. It *is* moving toward you. Now would be the time to turn to your new friend in alarm.

"I'm going to assume you've never been train-hopping before! Hold on tight! And when I say *jump*, jump!"

Take his hand.

Is he excited, or is he just yelling because the sound is growing exponentially louder around us? A bit of both, perhaps. Deafening noise, but a beautiful sound, like the breathing of the entire world at once.

Why, but it *is* a train!

It hurtles past you at remarkable speed, curving down from the sky and then upward again into the night. Look at your friend: oh dear, he's *saying* something, but you just can't hear it. Listen closely, *listen*. All these words, all the light in his eyes, all the spark in his gaze, all the stardust in his movements, but nothing can overcome the deafening roar.

"*Jump!*"

Well, come on. Do it!

The earth falls away; everything falls away from you, and now you are a shooting star in the sky. Light flashes past you in brilliant colors, brilliant shades of white and silver and gold. You can feel the light of a thousand suns shining in your own eyes; you can see the wind of a thousand moons in your breath.

You're on a train.

"There you go, steady."

Turn to him. Don't try to hide the grin on your face. The Nightwind Express. You're riding it.

"There's this trick, you see, but only if you're ready. See, you find a handle on the side like this. Grip it tight, and then—"

He leans out into the night, smile winkling like just another star. He lets out a yell.

Should you do it? Of course you should. Silly question.

Reach for a handle. That's it. Hold it tight, real tight. Two hands, if you must. It's all right to be scared. But you have to do it anyway.

Swing yourself away from the train and into the sea of lights. Feel the sigh of the universe. Listen to the song of everything.

Think: *I am above. There is nothing hanging over me. Everything that is near me I choose, and everything else is beneath. Someday I might get off this train, and my feet will touch the ground again. Someday I will be beneath, I will be amongst, and I will be between. But I will always remember the moment that I overcame it all. I will always remember this moment because right now I am ABOVE.*

Sherry Joyce

Formerly a Silicon Valley vice president of human resources, author Sherry Joyce enjoyed many years of creative and technical writing, from product marketing to serving as editor-in-chief of high-tech company newsletters. Allied-, ASID- and NKBA-credentialed, Sherry is the owner of SJDesigns Interiors.

 Her award-winning projects and articles have been featured in *Gentry*, *Builder Architect*, *California Home and Design*, *National Kitchen and Bath*, and the university textbook *Fundamentals of Interior Design*.

She is a member of Sacramento Sisters in Crime, Northern California Publishers & Authors, San Francisco Women's Book Association and Romance Writers of America.

Sherry Joyce's debut fiction, *The Dordogne Deception*, was conceived when the tower of the French chateau where she was vacationing was struck by lightning. She enjoys travel with her husband and spoiling her beloved Westies, Daisy and Kelsey.

SHERRY JOYCE
Cozumel Calamity

There are vacations from heaven, and there are vacations from the depths of hell.

Older and wiser, I now know not to book a vacation from a brochure devoid of any actual photographs of the resort—which is exactly what we did. We were young. We were trusting and foolish enough to believe the anonymous glowing comments in the brochure for Caribe Club Cozumel—the diving paradise where the Kennedy family had vacationed. We figured the Caribe Club Cozumel, with such a prestigious clientele, was a five-star (or at least a four-star) resort. In retrospect, we're simply glad to be alive to tell about the most hideous and hilarious adventure six friends could endure.

We dozed on the uneventful flight to Cozumel, Mexico, dreaming of a luxurious vacation replete with pristine beaches and spectacular sunsets. The taxi ride to the resort was an ominous portent of events to come. Flipped-over washing machines and decaying appliances scattered alongside the road beside gigantic, rusted, garbage dumpsters and odd remnants of past hurricanes. Eternally optimistic, we believed we'd turn the next corner and arrive at our luxurious resort.

We arrived at the pool, suitcases in tow and Panama hats on our heads. The look on my brother-in-law's face is now a family legend. Instead of a gregarious welcome, his somber, red-eyed expression alarmed us. "What's wrong?" we asked, concerned that someone had become ill or worse. "Everything!" Frank stammered in a guttural laugh that alarmed both my husband and me.

Watching guests lounging by the hotel's pool set off the first alarm bell. Swimmers had slathered on plenty of suntan lotion to avoid the broil of sunburns so easy to acquire near the equator. With disgust, we noticed that most of the lotion was swirling on the surface of the pool, an uninviting, milky, slimy, oil slick. It was obvious no filter or chlorine existed to sanitize either the swimmers' suntan lotion or bodily events children might've left behind.

Undiscouraged, we agreed we would check into our rooms and then meet up for a drink. Our ground-level room with aqua floor-tiles was pleasant enough but equipped with two sagging twin beds. However, I noticed a worrisome gap between the exterior door and the floor, large enough for small rodents to sneak in during the night. We set our bags down and headed outside to the pool area. Still dismayed, Frank suggested we try to get into another resort, the El Presidente, proclaiming the Caribe Club Cozumel a "low-end $320/night hovel." Our dear friends, Bill and Dianne, already sun-blistered from a short nap poolside, agreed we should look at another resort option. Sister-in-law Christina was silent and depressed, already loopy from the margaritas she'd swallowed upon arrival. Five disillusioned adults in search of a high-end resort piled into the rental car.

The drive to the next resort was as bumpy and bone-shaking as our initial ride to the Caribe Club Cozumel. Apparently potholed streets were not supposed to be re-paved over after hurricane destruction. The roads afforded both the driver and passengers automatic spinal adjustments. Who needs a chiropractor in Cozumel?

The alternative resort presented itself as a much lovelier establishment. But the fact that none of the toilets were working (they would not be fixed for days) was inauspicious. Stinky toilets were not acceptable, nor were the sounds of the huge construction crane next door. The crane lethargically moved dirt and concrete around in pointless circles. We all agreed we would have to make the best of it back at Caribe Club Cozumel.

One reason we'd booked our stay at Caribe Club Cozumel was their touted, twenty-first century, water-filtration plant. Clever us, we'd assured ourselves we wouldn't succumb to Montezuma's Revenge on this vacation. My husband and I walked through the resort to check out the advertised filtration plant. Massive cables lay uselessly on the floor. With no evidence of electricity, we quickly realized the filtration device was neither plugged in nor operable. We vowed to drink only canned drinks and try our darnedest to remain healthy during our stay in Mexico.

Bedtime arrived. Reluctant to shut off the lights and fearful about the gap under the exterior room's door, I grabbed three minuscule towels from the bathroom (I noticed the yellow stains and the lack of fluffiness) and stuffed them under the door. During the night, a trip to the bathroom was necessary. Apprehensive of crawling bugs, I turned on the night-stand lamp between our twin beds—and screamed. A cockroach the size of a frankfurter sat in the middle of the small white rug, its antennae wiggling back and forth and devil eyes flicking at me. Jim jumped up, saw my pale face, and grabbed his size-fourteen shoe, intent on splattering the roach to death. But fast little buggers they are. *Whomp, whomp, swat, whack*—missed it! The hideous insect scampered up the bed leg and squeezed under the mattress. Horrified, I threatened to take the next plane home. Jim lifted the mattresses. No roach in sight. My husband persuaded me the bug had scampered into the wall somewhere. If we left all the lights on in the room, he told me, the cockroach would not reappear—and the Easter Bunny was real too!

After a restless night, sleeping with one eye open, I detected dawn seeping through the faded curtains. I looked forward to a hot shower and headed cautiously to the bathroom. I carefully scanned the floor for bugs and rodents. Jim slept soundly in his bed, tired from his nocturnal bug-whomping and mattress-antics.

Sleep-deprived, I climbed into the shower and grabbed the shower bar, inadvertently sliding the shower door from one side of the tub to the other. Terrified, I felt the entire door come off in my hands nearly toppling me onto the floor. More screaming. Jim bolted from bed, expecting to see me smacking bugs. Instead, my husband was astounded to see the sight of his wife balancing a glass shower door over her head, arms shaking with the weight. Assessing the situation, Jim grabbed the shower door and carefully set it on the floor. I wish the shower door had not come off because the sight of the grungy shower tiles was repulsive. I scraped my finger across the tile wondering how long the maid had been blind. After a trickling shower and drying off with a towel the size of a bath mat, I walked over to the bed noticing giant, yellow stains on the sheets. Had they been there for days? Weeks? Months? What, pray tell, what was the maid delivering each day? Dirty sheets? Too depressed to think about it, we headed to the dining room for breakfast.

Looking for our group in the dining room, we were happy to greet our dear friend, Dianne. Where was her husband, Bill? Dianne said he was not feeling well and would be late for breakfast. Frank arrived with Christina, who said she would not be eating either because her stomach burbled with volcanic activity. A buffet beckoned those of us who were hungry, but also surprised us because we could not recognize any of the food. Everything was either breaded and deep-fried or covered with tomato sauce. I learned grouper was the only offering I could stomach. I would quickly learn to despise it.

The hotel situated its tennis courts adjacent to the ocean. Our group agreed to play together as soon as Bill made his appearance. We were avid tennis players and looking forward to a competitive game.

We headed back to change into tennis attire, walking past the main reception desk to find enraged patrons screaming obscenities at the desk clerk. The twelve-story hotel structure was not only without water but also without working elevators. During a lull in the heated exchanges, we asked where we could find pay phones were. The staff responded nonplused and uncooperative, as though our request was to call Greenland instead of nearby California.

Jim vociferously complained to the desk clerk who was fielding swatting arms of disgruntled guests. He simply nodded and shrugged his shoulders as if selective deafness were a welcome affliction. Copper had been stolen from the pay phone wires years ago, and it might take five days before we could make a phone call. No TV, no telephone, no desirable food, a bug-infested room with stained-sheets, a non-working shower door on the floor, and the anticipation of an abundance of fleshy, smelly grouper—who could complain? Even stuck in less-than-paradise, the warm weather and beautiful ocean was a treat. This was not the worst that could happen—or was it?

Arriving at the tennis court (just one), our friends burst into hysterics. The net had sagged to one foot off of the ground. Basketball-sized holes pocked the surface. The court was parallel to the ocean and not more than two feet from the sand and incoming waves. Our mirth burbled over when we saw the court lacked fenced walls to keep the tennis ball inside. Stomachs aching with laughter, we agreed two of us could play while the other four players stood guard on the sides to whack the ball back into play so it would not go spinning off into the ocean. Six people playing a four-sided game of tennis was pants-splitting fun. Sometimes the ball went out of bounds. It either sank into the ocean or flew completely off the court into the pile of dilapidated roofing tiles. At one point, I tried to grab an errant tennis ball only to see an iguana the size of a small child crawl out from the roof tiles. He tested my resolve about how badly I wanted the ball. An exhausting game of six-person tennis ended in laughter and us starving for lunch. As we departed the court, an iguana waddled behind us, like a pet dog.

Starved for eggs—or a salad—I carefully reminded myself not to eat anything that might have been washed in local water. I assumed lunch would be different from breakfast, but no, the same buffet appeared: the same breaded, strategically disguised food and plenty of tomato-slathered grouper.

We were stuck in a resort without phones, but at least we had water and resided in the resort's two-story building. We pitied those patrons walking up twelve flights of stairs without a phone to get off the island. We were better off! We would salvage this vacation and develop character! We would not succumb to despair! Making a conscious decision not to be miserable, we began to laugh at every mishap.

The following morning Bill failed to show up for breakfast, lunch or dinner. Frank, the dentist, had brought medicinal drugs for severe "trots," and we visited Bill in his room. He lay flat out on the bed, praying for death. His wife became the psychotic nurse Ratched (somehow fitting) from *One Flew Over The Cuckoo's Nest*, dutifully checking each of our rooms with Doctor Frank each morning, assessing who among us had succumbed to Montezuma's Revenge. It quickly became necessary for Jim and Frank to go to town for more medicine and stomach aids. Standing in the drugstore, Jim looked down at the newspaper pile on the floor and spewed a barrage of four-letter words. He'd seen the headline, "American Stores does a Leveraged Buyout of Lucky Stores." Jim stood, shocked and livid because his company had been sold during the time he was being deprived of good food and local telephones. Did he still have a job? Could he call and find out if he would be working in Utah instead of California? No, he would have to wait four more days until copper could be replaced in the telephone cables. If ever there were ever a reason to drink, this was it. Day-by-day we would become alcoholics. That's how we'd manage our remaining eight days of Caribe Club hell.

Gradually we went native. We accepted our slimy pool and basked in the sun, drinking neon beverages with tiny umbrellas until we could no longer form words. I begged Jim to move us to the second-floor rooms because, logically, it would take that much longer for the roaches to climb to the second story. Seeing our new room with its view of the ocean, I was momentarily comforted— until I saw the floor-to-ceiling volcanic rock wall across the room, chock-full of massive holes. Perfect hiding spaces for roaches. The maid's face was bemused when she arrived the next morning. We must've been the most eccentric hotel guests she'd encountered. We'd moved the bed to the middle of the room (we didn't want to be under the ceiling fan because Bill had gotten an electric shock the day before from the live dangling wires) and, because the rock wall was breeding crawling things, I'd stuffed every crack with toilet paper. The entire rock wall was paper white instead of lava black. At least my sanity was intact!

Making the most of our stay in Cozumel, we laughed non-stop, drank more than we ate, and managed a ninety-foot dive in exceptionally clear water that was as warm at ninety feet deep as it was at the surface. Sharks had not eaten us that day. Life was good. Hungry from the dive, we all agreed to go to dinner to celebrate our survival of yet one more day in "paradise." The Mariachi band played, and we were enjoying dinner when—gasp—we were nearly decapitated. An enormous fan broke loose from the ceiling, sailed through the dining room, and landed on the floor. The band played on! Apparently, this was a frequent occurrence. We ordered several more drinks and shook our heads in disbelief. We changed our resort's moniker to Stinkin' Caribe Club Cozumel. Not one person in the dining room blinked an eye. Aghast, we looked at the ceiling fan, mangled under the table leg where bloody heads, arms, and legs could have been. Zombie patrons simply stepped over the blades and kept on dancing. I asked Jim to slap me hard so that I might wake up.

One more day and we would all be going home. That night we saw a guest on his stomach, crawling to his room. We offered help while he giggled, grunted, and slithered. Laughing in fellowship with the hapless crawling guest, we figured he'd been there longer than we had. If we stayed, we too would undoubtedly end up in a flat-out, stomach-crawling drunken stupor.

Dianne, Jim, and I rented a jeep to tour the island's historic ruins. We learned it had been Joe and Ethel Kennedy who'd stayed at the resort, and that it had immediately slipped into receivership and disrepair after they left. The Caribe Club's rental jeep was darling, sporting a pink-and-white striped, scalloped-fringed canopy. Jim elected to drive, and Dianne sat up front. I reluctantly climbed into the back seat. Several potholed bounces, a vehicle tilt and... boom! We broke into laughter when the side-view mirrors collapsed and now hung vertically to the ground. Without rearview or side-view mirrors, Jim could not see anything behind us. We maneuvered the potholes as though they were landmines, unable to go forward or backward. Thankfully, a rearview mirror was not needed. No other tourists were dumb enough to try this adventure. Being stranded in desolation became a possibility. I had not noticed the sock in the gas tank before. Would that explode? Suddenly we hit a giant pothole, and the entire upper canopy collapsed on Jim and Dianne's head, landing in their laps. Not only could the front-seat driver and rider not see behind them, but they could also no longer see forward either. Driving blind took on new meaning as we maneuvered with gut-splitting laughter.

Arriving at the historical site was anticlimactic. The ruins were ruined, barely visible Mayan remnants. Homeward bound meant revisiting the potholes again and tossing the canopy in the backseat to keep me company. How long had we been on this vacation? Months? Years?

Although ten days seemed an eternity, the last blissful day had finally arrived. Jim found out he still had a job—in fact he had two, one with the Lucky Stores and one with the American Stores. Bill and Dianne survived without requiring hospitalization. Frank and Christina, on the brink of divorce, headed home early. With a sigh of relief, Dianne and I sat on her balcony, looking at the sea and watching windsurfers pulled haphazardly by the unswimmable ocean's undertow. Coast Guard boats zoomed to retrieve desperate, panicked windsurfers, now separated from their boards. This was our daily entertainment—watching windsurfers, one-by-one, attempt and fail navigation of the powerful undercurrent.

Looking up the coast, I shouted, "What *is* that?" An enormous, green, monstrous slime was rapidly engulfing the sea, flooding the swimming areas. That was it. The grand finale. We picked up our oversized drinks and toasted our final day at the Caribe Club Cozumel—the worst and best vacation, ever.

Thirty years later, Dianne and I still laugh about the experience. Jim's brother still wears the badge of honor for dentistry medicine he'd brought in his black valise that saved some of us from death-by-dirty-water. Honest with myself, I sometimes muse that the vacation could not have been as bad as the details that linger in my memory. Then I slap myself back to reality—knowing it was much, much worse.

Sharon S. Darrow

A Sacramento business woman, Sharon S. Darrow is also the author of three books. She has published *Bottlekatz, a Complete Care Guide for Orphan Kittens*, which serves as a training manual for rescue groups.

Her book *From Hindsight to Insight; A Traditional to Metaphysical Memoir* was born out of her desire to share a deeply held conviction that nothing in life is an acci-dent and that everyone receives subtle guidance throughout their lives.

Her third book, *Faces of Rescue; Cats, Kittens and Great Danes* contains stories about rescued kittens, cats, great Danes, and the people who do rescue work.

Sharon serves as president of Northern California Publishers and Authors, and she maintains a writers' resource website, at SacWritersAlliance. com. Her small business, Travel ID Cards, markets identification cards for child travel and custom cards for companies, organizations, and events.

Visit her website at www.sharonsdarrow.com, and enjoy her insightful blog comments at this address: sharonsdarrow.wordpress.com.

SHARON S. DARROW
Fragile Dreams

I have no idea how young I was when I started dreaming about flying. The dreams were magic and private, the perfect soothing prelude to falling asleep every night. I'd curl up in bed, covers tightly tucked around my neck and close my eyes to escape into my own special meadow surrounded by giant trees. I always wore a simple dress, white socks, and Mary Jane shoes. A soft, warm breeze lifted long, curly, red hair off my neck until I raised my arms up over my head and leaped up into the air.

I soared effortlessly, Superman style, hair streaming back from my head, dress stretched modestly along my legs as I skimmed above the treetops just seconds after takeoff. Each flight, each dream, was perfect. The sun was a warm caress against my skin. A soft breeze was always gentle and comforting against my body, and the trees below were all perfectly shaped evergreens. Flight was effortless, zooming upwards towards the clouds, then diving and twisting until I skimmed just above the ground. Then I would climb back up, executing acrobatic turns and loops, sometimes just hovering like a lazy dragonfly in the summer air. When I was ready to rest for a moment, I'd glide gently down onto a huge tree branch where I could rest my back against the sturdy trunk. I'd stay there, swaying in the wind, watching animals pass under the tree completely unaware of my gaze. After a while, I'd leap back up, soaring in the sun until the dream carried me into deep, peaceful sleep.

I had the same dream night after night and found it incredibly comforting. It was my favorite way to put myself to sleep, especially if the day had ended with trouble in the house from fighting between my parents or my brothers. I can remember getting lost in the sensations of the dream until it felt more real than the bed and pillow I rested on. Sometimes I'd go to bed to escape tension in the household, deliberately closing my eyes and leaping into the air to find tranquility not available anywhere else.

For years, the flying dreams were my special secret, shared with no one. I didn't tell my brothers because they'd have laughed at me, and I kept the secret from my parents because they wouldn't have understood. I still don't know what compelled me to open up one day and share my dreams with a teacher.

As an oldest child, with three younger brothers, I always had lots of responsibilities at home. My place in the family meant helping around the house, helping to care for my siblings, and trying not to create any additional stress for my parents. I never doubted my parents love, but I knew they didn't have time to spend dealing with any difficulties I might be having. Consequently I tried hard to solve problems for myself, and the soothing flying dreams were an enormous comfort.

Then I started school and loved it from the very first day. Learning came easy for me, which meant teachers were quick and lavish with praise and hugs. Teachers became my new heroes, and from day one I was always one of their favorites. Yes, teacher's pet from the start, but the approval and attention to a child who had never felt special was amazing. My parents taught me to respect my elders and authority figures, and that early lesson compounded my admiration and affection for teachers.

One day after class I decided to share my flying dreams with a trusted teacher, a woman I liked. It was like giving her a special, personal gift that would enhance our bond of affection and trust. To my utter shock, the teacher gave me a disgusted look and said, "That's crazy. You know people can't fly!" I still remember feeling betrayed and hurt by her reaction but said nothing back to her. There were simply no words to express the sadness that overwhelmed me. I spent the rest of the day numb, unable to understand the teacher's response.

That night, as soon as I crawled into bed, my mind in turmoil, I closed my eyes and immediately found myself in the familiar sunny meadow. Needing the peace my dream always brought, I reached my hands up, bent my knees and tried to leap into the air. For the first time ever, it didn't work. No matter how hard I tried, my feet remained firmly attached to the ground. I can still remember feeling an incredible, profound sense of loss at finding myself unable to soar into the sky. Instead of the treasured tranquility of my dream, all I felt was the awful finality and truth of that teacher's words.

Many times in the weeks, months, and years to come I'd remember my dream, but was never able to recapture the feeling. I'd sometimes try to conjure up some new flying dream but was never able to imagine myself getting off the ground. I eventually stopped trying to fly in my dreams but never stopped grieving for what I'd lost.

Then one day as an adult I finally absorbed the message that we all create and shape our own worlds through our imagination, desires, and belief. I'm sure I'd heard and read the same thing many times, from multiple sources, but it finally hit home. At last I dared to believe that my mind, my world, my imagination were under my control. No one else's negative words had power over me without my permission.

That night I waited until everyone else in the house was asleep, then closed my eyes and imagined myself in the meadow of my childhood dream. I reached my arms up above my head and leaped up into the air. To my amazement I went straight up above the trees, then flew like an arrow right up to the clouds. Then I drifted down onto a branch of the tallest tree and rested against the trunk. Incredible! Not only could I fly in my dreams again, but I also reconnected with the same incredible sense of peace.

When I regained my ability to dream of flying, I also grasped the enormous power of the words we use. My teacher might have been more sensitive and tactful when she told me people couldn't fly, but I'm sure she had no idea of the devastating effect her words had. This personal experience taught me how easily a dream can be crushed by a thoughtless phrase, and how difficult it can be to regain it.

Joyce Mason

J oyce Mason is a prolific writer and astrologer. She has authored hundreds of articles and five books on astrology and metaphysical topics.

In 2013, she added fiction to the mix with *The Crystal Ball*, the first in her Micki Michaels mystery series. Her literary trademark—delivering depth insights with humor—crosses several genres.

When not writing literal mysteries, Joyce writes  about the mysteries of life. She's got more Micki adventures and a memoir in store.

Visit her website at www.joycemason.com to learn more.

JOYCE MASON
Valley Girl

O f all the traditional prayers I have ever known, the Twenty-Third Psalm is my favorite. It's my number-one, even
though it's mostly quoted at funerals. The association between "The Lord is my shepherd" and death felt morbid until I
realized how much we live at death's door all the time. That makes
it a prayer for all seasons and reasons. I love it, especially this line:

*Yea, though I walk through the Valley of the Shadow of Death, I will
fear no evil, for Thou art with me. Thy rod and thy staff, they comfort me.*

Who couldn't use a rod, maybe even a tire iron, especially in a
bad neighborhood? (A 'hood where Death lurks definitely qualifies
as bad.) As a card-carrying member of AARP, I'd want a rod that's
long enough to double as a walking stick in case my arthritic knee
caves. That way, when my rod's not in service as a handy weapon
to scare off the need for actual self-defense, it could keep me from
falling on my face or tripping over my tongue.

And I'd really like a staff. You know, a few personal assistants
to help me organize my complicated life. But handy tools and
divine intervention aside, I've been thinking more often in my ac-
cumulating years just how vulnerable we are as human beings. We
have this thin layer of skin separating our fragile innards from all
sorts of collisions with germs, crazies, cars, trees, and rabid dogs.
The number of things that could keep people from making it to
their country's average lifespan is frightening. It was frightening
before 9/11; now add the potential for domestic terror.

As we get older, the Shadow of Death gets thicker. It goes

from partly cloudy to seriously overcast as you inch toward the un-known finish line of life. There are only two options. Get bummed or do what you did when you were a kid—get your thrills from liv-ing on the edge. After spending considerable time in the darkening Valley, you might discover that you suffer from Seasonal Affective Disorder (SAD), that condition from too little sunshine. If so, sit yourself under a full-spectrum light several times a day, a metaphor for lightening up through humor, insight, spirit, or the light bulbs of learning.

If I could only have one T-shirt with a message to sum up my attitude toward life, it'd say, "Gutsy." I don't do roller coasters anymore, but I do life in America in my 60s. That's braver than the Bobs at Riverview. When I was growing up in Chicago, that 90-degree-drop coaster was our Superman Ride of Steel. It takes even more guts to keep living life to the max, doing work you love, and constantly loving to learn, especially when your body is show-ing wear. I don't see any other realistic alternative.

The game of life is to live as long as you can, as well as you can. While we haven't conquered physical death, there is no death in spirit, so my recommendation is to live, laugh and love to the end. Live like there's no tomorrow. Someday there won't be. Don't regret anything. If you do, hurry up and fix it.

That's why I'm a Valley Girl. I know I live in the Valley of the Shadow of Death, but when you think about it, we have lived here all of our lives. It's miraculous that anyone makes it through childhood, especially puberty. Kids think they are invincible. They fly from trees and on skateboards. They take up sports that should all have the same name, Accident Waiting to Happen. It only gets worse once a driver's license gives them access to cars as could-be lethal weapons.

As we mature, we know better. We understand how vulnera-ble we are, but we shouldn't act like it. Sure, maybe we could avoid skydiving—maybe not. At a minimum, we should retain a child-like, adventurous spirit and be brave heroes of our own lives, even if we know death could be crouching around any corner ready to spring. The ever-present Shadow is a reminder, maybe a nag, to live life to the fullest.

Don't let statistics scare you, either. The ones I found say American men live on average to 77, their female counterparts to

82. You are not a statistic. How each of us will fare in this lotto of life, we just don't know. Even when family history offers some hints, genes are not everything. There are other factors, and the true shadows in the Valley are the vast maybes—the delicious and dismaying uncertainties of life.

We are fortunate to live much longer than our grandparents. We're among the first to get this much time as the rule, rather than the exception. What's more, we are the first to get to figure out what to do with our extra time. Except I don't seem to have any. That's the irony. I always feel like I'm playing that old '50s quiz show game, *Beat the Clock*, even in so-called retirement or semi-retirement. (Baby boomers don't retire because they only know how to do. They don't know how to just be.) We live in an era of time acceleration, thanks to communication tools that are so instantaneous, the domino effect of so much interaction creates more and faster action—more ideas, more to-do lists, and more bombardment of stimuli.

If you don't believe me that we're living longer, go browse some greeting cards. Recently at the drugstore, I found several selections for the milestone birthdays 90 and 100! My oldest living relative on my mother's side is 88, on my father's side, 96. I hope the fact that I need to buy these cards bodes well for me.

Despite all the possible perils, most of us are going to last, so how do we make the most of it? The answer is in your own history. You don't have to wait till you "go to the light" to let your life flash in front you. Examine your key life events, study our patterns, and discover the themes and lessons of your personal drama. The show to date contains the prescription for a cool rest of your life. The tools are intuition, insight, and dogged analysis. It's like a fabulous whodunit in which you are both star and detective with the outcome unknown—only instead of the usual stiff in the early scenes, you're trying to live out loud and avoid becoming one any sooner than you have to. The coolest part of this exercise is that you have a lot of control over the action. You can write a snoring bore, a romantic comedy, or a thriller that keeps you on the edge of your seat.

Think like a movie critic, review your life, and if you aren't getting five stars and the deeper symbolism, visit the chopping block and edit. More than ever, we live in a world of constant change. Whatever change we need, help is within easy reach. Opportunities to grow and tools to do are unprecedented.

When I say, "examine your life," I mean in time as we know it. I have no interest in going *Back to the Future*, although it was a delightful movie. Too complicated.

My fantasy, instead, involves some pill or potion—maybe a hotline to heaven—that would give me a glimmer of how the world would have been without me. I want that transformative trip Jimmy Stewart took in *It's a Wonderful Life*. The closest you ever get to hearing what you were good for, good at, or what good you did is at your own funeral. That's a day late and a compliment short.

I propose, instead, this alternative for a big-number birthday. Throw yourself a living memorial, a fun funeral that you can attend, not as a discarnate entity, but right in your own body. Write your own obituary on the cover of the invitations and challenge folks to say nice things about you to your face while you can still hear them. Everyone can wear black, and if you're really campy, you can even lie in a coffin while the speeches take place, although I'd double dare you to not move a muscle, laugh, or cry during this spectacle. Of course, an Irish wake must be held, complete with abundant booze and bawdy jokes. An embarrassing video is mandatory.

When my husband and I renewed our vows in a church wedding nine years after eloping, I considered planting a skeleton couple on our cake, Day-of-the-Dead style. I found the figurines in a local import shop, and the Bonies are hilarious in their bride-and-groom garb. He was actually okay with this idea, but my bent for beauty ruled, and I opted for fresh flowers instead. Maybe the death-defying figurines will take the cake on our silver wedding anniversary when we're 75 just before our joint, living funeral. We were born in the same month, same year; we'd just have to fake death at the same time.

I first discovered the expression "*live fast, die young, and leave a good-looking corpse*" when I was a teenager in some book I can no longer identify. I have Googled it to death (no pun intended), and all I can find is that everyone wants to take or give credit for the slogan with no authentication. I have an alternative catchphrase I live by: *Live large—and die as cool, late and good-looking as you can.*

There was a Bob Hope movie (1951), *The Lemon Drop Kid*, in

which the comedian played a con man with a scheme that involved a home for "old dolls." It's a Christmas flick, and aside from introducing the classic tune *Silver Bells*, I think Bob had the right attitude toward female seniors. Granted, you might consider *doll* a little sexist (consider the era, not the ERA), but he was implying they were still luscious. I just got the pun, too...*silver belles*!

The greatest gift of my complicated hysterectomy in my mid-40s, aside from igniting hot flashes of insight about my own life's movie, was my brush with death. I had a chance to learn that, in the end, I'd be okay with whatever time I've got because I have lived life to the hilt every day. Still, there are certain things I feel I must do before dying. Writing books is one of them—the main one. Half the time, while writing, I feel the Grim Reaper breathing down my neck. Writing my bucket list has given me a lot of anxiety—like, once I check off all the items, will I automatically keel over?

Really, all I want is to be ready—or at least willing—to let go and be flooded with love, just like I felt back in the hospital during my close brush in 1992. There life and death merged into the obvious continuum and made the reason for living with passion clear. In the same spirit, my favorite spiritual guidance on life came from a pastor during Lent. He was addressing the Catholic custom of giving up something you enjoy as a sacrifice in the weeks leading up to Easter. Father Wise One said God doesn't give a rip about our relationship with chocolate (what a relief to this unrepentant chocoholic). He invited us, instead, to do more of what puts a sparkle in our eye, because "that's of God." That's passion, what sets us on fire, what makes us more alive and brings fulfillment.

Whatever your faith or whatever you call the force that created and constantly recreates and renews you (feel free to substitute your own terms), the Twenty-Third Psalm is the ultimate affirmation that the circle is never broken. This is the most comforting fact we will ever know. It is enough to put a sparkle, maybe even a tear, in anyone's eye:

Surely, goodness and mercy will follow me all the days of my life, and I will dwell in the house of the Lord forever.

C.T. Meadows

Ever since she was fifteen years old, C.T Meadows wanted to be a writer.

Her first career began as a police dispatcher, but once women were permitted to become cops, she became a police officer. She found it a colorful and interesting lifestyle and has many tales to tell about it.

In her next career, she became a day-spa own-er. She had a beautiful and quaint little shop with superb services. She was a licensed as a massage therapist, aesthetician, manicurist, and hypnotherapist.

C.T. has begun a new journey—to finally fulfill her life-long dream to become a writer. Though she's only published short stories thus far, she is a prolific writer and is currently working on more than one novel.

Writing is one of the things she loves most, besides doo-wop music and dancing the tango.

C.T. MEADOWS

Legend of the Mountain
Colorado Mountains, 1850

Stay the winter in this worthless mine? You must be crazy!" Dawson shouted. "Those wretches who sold us this mine must've seeded it, because we haven't found enough gold to buy even supplies. I'm tired of hacking useless stones out of rock-hard dirt and tired of being cold and eating beans."

"Then get the hell out! I don't need your help. And don't come back beggin' when I make it big, either!" Hezekiah stomped to the other side of the mine, sat down next to the camp-stove and guzzled whiskey.

Dawson knew the tiny stove was all that kept them from freezing to death. When it got below freezing outside, they even shared the small space with their mules.

"You shouldn't stay here alone, Hezekiah. It's too dangerous. Remember that old-timer telling us about that crazed grizzly that follows trappers and miners like he's hunting them down to kill?"

"Just cause you're scare't, don't mean I can't take care of myself. I ain't no coward like you."

"I was just warning you for your own good. Last time we were in town, another miner told me to keep a sharp eye out for that grizzly. Claimed he saw it across the river once. Said it only had one ear and looked to be over a thousand pounds of pure hell. Big enough to tear a horse apart easy.

"Besides, you don't have enough supplies or ammunition to spend the rest of the winter here. You're liable to freeze to death in a blizzard and have to eat your mules just to survive."

"Why don't you mind your own business and quit tryin' to tell me how to live, like you know everythin'."

"'Cause you're too dumb to understand you could die up here, and I don't want that on my conscience. But have it your way. I'm leaving in the morning."

Without answering, Hezekiah reached out and snagged his bedroll, dragged it over himself, and was snoring within minutes.

The next morning Dawson woke him. "Hey, you sure you don't want to go?"

Hezekiah grumbled, "No. Damn it. Now leave me alone," and turned over, covering his head.

Dawson walked outside and looked around at the dirty, miserable mining camp, glad to be leaving all this hardship behind. Gusting winds had blown most of the leaves off the aspens, making the place look more barren and dismal than ever. Even the freshly fallen snow couldn't beautify its ugliness.

It was bitterly cold, and another snowstorm looked to be moving in. He saddled Snapper, his best mule, packed another with supplies and rode off down the trail.

***

As Dawson left camp, he didn't see the bushes and tree limbs of the pines moving apart behind him, or the huge grizzly stand up on its hind legs and sniff the air just outside the mine's opening. The bear watched Dawson ride downhill, but the familiar smell of man drifting from the dark open space drew his attention away.

***

Last night Dawson had heard a lone wolf howl nearby and was glad no others answered the mournful cry. He hadn't heard of any wolf attacks but wanted no part of being the first to run into a hungry wolf pack.

He'd been traveling for hours and only stopped briefly at a stream around noon. Sundown was approaching, and Dawson was thirsty. For the past several miles both mules had been acting agitated. He figured they were tired and thirsty, too.

When he'd first left home, all he could think about was striking it rich. He'd never dreamed it could turn out any other way.

Going home broke and facing his father would be difficult.

Thinking about that—not focusing on things at hand—was how he'd missed the trail to the river. Dawson knew it was somewhere to his right and guided the mules onto the next downhill path that looked as if it might lead there. Within minutes, he heard the loud, bubbling water as it flowed rapidly over the rocky riverbed.

He needed to set up camp soon. He saw plenty of wood lying about to make a fire to keep the wild animals and cold at bay.

As he traveled through the pines, snowflakes began falling, like flour through a sifter, covering the ground in white powder. It would be a long, miserable night if the snow continued. The woods had become utterly still and silent, except for the rattling of supplies on the pack-mule, the sound of hoof-beats, and the jingling of reins.

Suddenly the pack-mule began a high-pitched hee-hawing, jerking around wildly.

That's when the big, one-eared grizzly rose up on its hind feet and grasped the mule's haunches with his great paws. Dawson dropped the lead rope as the pack-mule kicked hard and raced away, squealing in pain and fear. Dawson yanked out his heavy rifle. He turned toward the charging bear, aimed, and fired.

The bullet slammed into the bear, jerking its shoulder back. Unstopped, the grizzly stood up, roared, and clutched Dawson's mule by the neck. Snapper thrashed his head back and forth, trying to rear up and use his hooves to fight for his life, but the bear was too strong and powerful.

Dawson reached for his pistol, trying to stay in the saddle as Snapper screeched hee-haws, kicking and flailing to free himself from the demon's hold.

When the mule crashed to the ground, Dawson's leg was trapped underneath and instantly snapped. He couldn't afford to pass out now. With monumental effort, he grabbed the big hunting knife from his belt, just as the injured bear grabbed onto him.

Dawson ducked to avoid the bear's snapping teeth and stabbed the grizzly's soft underbelly fast and hard repeatedly, struggling to kill the beast before it ripped him to pieces. The bear bled profusely but wasn't weakening quickly enough.

Dawson spotted his handgun nearby. He grabbed it, firing

blindly several times. Suddenly, the grizzly dropped him and stumbled away.

The gashes on Dawson's shoulders, arms, and back were bad, but his mule was in worse shape. Snapper was writhing in the throes-of-death. Dawson used his last shot to end the mule's suffering, not realizing he should have kept it in case the rogue bear returned.

He crawled over to Snapper's back to pull a bedroll and extra shirt from behind the saddle. Dawson tore off pieces of the shirt, hastily stuffed them over his wounds, and tugged the bedroll around himself as best he could. Shivering badly, he laid against the dead mule to block the brutal wind and blowing snow.

Dawson remembered listening to the mournful howl of a wolf the night before and hoped none were close. His last thought before losing consciousness was that the smell of blood might draw other wild animals.

***

The grizzly struggled along, leaving a cherry-red swathe of blood on the snowy white ground, trailing his every step. He huffed and grunted, his breathing ragged.

Otherwise, the forest was eerily quiet as if aware of the humongous creature's suffering and his life's energies draining away along with his blood.

But a lone wolf, not fully grown, had not heard the warning signals of the silent forest or noticed the lack of creatures moving about. He'd been wandering around sniffing for a mate.

The young wolf trotted around the corner of a large boulder and came face to face with the dying bear. The wolf yipped in surprise at the closeness of the fierce predator, instinctively realizing his life was in danger.

The grizzly reacted violently and furiously, striking the yelping wolf with the last of his strength as if the wolf had caused his wounds and pain. When the bear's heart finally stopped, he collapsed, relinquishing his hold on the battered and torn creature.

The wolf rose shakily, still bleeding, and stumbled away.

His distorted vision made it difficult to seek water, but an unquenchable thirst drove him to follow the scent and sound of the nearby river.

As the wolf got closer, he recognized the smell of fresh blood, yet heard no sound of an animal eating its kill. Then he noticed a scent he'd not encountered before. Confused, but desperate for water, he moved slowly toward the river.

***

Dawson was awakened during the night by the sound of a wolf's oddly strangled howling, then fell back into a miserably cold and troubled sleep. The next morning he woke in agony from his broken leg. His other wounds were painful but bearable and bleeding less.

He felt the peculiar sensation of being watched, then heard faint footsteps moving his direction. The predawn light wasn't bright enough to see clearly. Dawson squinted to see what was coming and watched as a lone wolf hesitantly approached. The wolf moved oddly as if there were something wrong with it. Dawson noticed the animal was wobbling and shaking and hoped it wasn't rabid.

With Dawson's last bit of energy, he pulled the rifle up beside him. He'd have to hit the wolf hard enough to kill it since there was no more ammunition. As soon as it was close enough, he whomped the wolf over the head.

Dawson couldn't tell whether the animal was dead or not, so he crawled closer to check. There were gouges across the wolf's head and paws, and one hip was slashed. The animal's wounds were badly swollen and seeping blood. He wondered if the wolf could've been attacked by the same grizzly that mauled him.

He realized the wolf had probably been trying to get to the river for water, just as he had earlier.

Unlike Dawson's mule, the wolf might have a chance to live. Seeing the wolf's suffering reminded him of his own shepherd, as it lay dying from a wildcat attack when Dawson was only ten. Misgivings about whether to kill the creature tormented him. The animal was already near death. It would be easy to end its life now. But Dawson hesitated, figuring the wolf wouldn't recover enough to do him any harm.

Dawson thought that if no other animal came to finish him off, he might survive through the night. So might the wolf. Since the wolf's injuries were similar in severity to his own, he decided to let nature run its course. The wolf would live or die, but not by his hand, unless it tried to attack him.

After struggling to find a straight tree limb, Dawson cut a length of the dead mule's reins, using it to strap his broken leg to the branch. He'd seen that done once and wasn't sure he'd gotten it right, but it would have to do. It might make the pain less excruciating, so he could crawl around gathering wood for a fire before his already numb fingers completely froze.

Dawson painfully dragged himself over to a large fallen tree, backed up against the trunk and broke branches into pieces. He was glad it had only snowed a little; it would've been too hard to start a fire.

During the day, he only moved to add wood to the fire, drifting in and out of healing naps.

By evening, his hunger was unbearable. Dawson hadn't eaten since early yesterday. As he sat staring at Snapper's body, he realized he had no other option. He'd have to cut up the dead mule or starve.

With a great deal of unease, Dawson cut off a chunk of its haunch and cooked it over the fire. He tossed a piece of meat in front of the wolf, where it lay on the opposite side of the fire, sleeping or dying. Dawson couldn't tell which.

When the wolf roused, he sniffed the meat and immediately devoured it as he turned his head toward the firelight, growling feebly between bites, but didn't move.

The next morning the animal forced his injured body up and struggled to the river's edge to drink. He wobbled back to his spot on the other side of the fire and plopped down, too exhausted to move.

Except for keeping the fire going and cooking the meat, Dawson was just as lethargic. Every time he cooked for himself, he tossed some to the wolf. The wolf opened his eyes, gulped down the meat between weak growls, but never approached Dawson.

On their third day, a ferocious storm came howling through the mountains swirling snow all around them. Dawson fed the fire the biggest branches he could heft up and throw onto the flames. He huddled against the fallen tree trunk and wrapped his blankets around himself, unsure he'd survive the severe winds and snowdrifts throughout the night.

He woke the next morning stiff and nearly frozen, opened his eyes to the brisk morning, with crystal blue skies, and nearly screamed like a woman.

A huge, mountain of a man was grabbing armfuls of tree-limbs, shaking the snow off, and tossing them onto the spot where the fire had gone out.

Dawson was surprised that he was still alive. The snow had covered him cocoon fashion, where he lay against the tree-trunk. Even the wolf was half surrounded in a white mound.

The wolf raised his head out of the snow, gained his feet, growled low, and limped into the woods. The trapper swung around and stared at the injured animal with blatant curiosity, pointed at the wolf, said something unintelligible, then smiled at Dawson.

The stranger spoke broken English with a heavy French accent. He piled wood several feet high for the fire as if he intended to build it big enough to warm the whole forest. Once the fire was blazing, the mountain-man rigged up a makeshift half-shelter with long tree branches covered with furs to contain the heat and block some of the wind. Dawson realized that if the Frenchman hadn't come along he would've never survived.

Looking around, Dawson was surprised to see his own pack-mule with all his supplies tied beside the Trapper's mules. Amazingly, the animal looked okay, other than the welted claw marks across its haunch.

Dawson found it hard to understand the Frenchman, but they managed to converse adding hand motions and half-words. The mountain-man indicated he'd found the loaded pack-mule and figured someone would be looking for it. He implied he'd followed the smell of the wood-smoke yesterday until it got too dark.

The trapper pointed out that Dawson's broken leg didn't look right and offered to fix it so it would heal better The Frenchman found a straight tree branch, hacked it into several pieces, then forced Dawson's leg bones back into the correct position. Dawson passed out from the pain but woke up to find his leg bound tightly with furs and securely tied to the wood.

While his body healed, the two men continued to share the cooked meat for the next few days. They regularly threw chunks of meat to the spot where the injured wolf came each day.

At first the wolf returned warily, snuck up close, grabbed the meat, and struggled to hurry back into the woods, growling between bites as usual. Gradually he began to slip in to get the meat, then leave, without growling. Eventually, the wolf began lying next to the fire, opposite the men, muzzle resting on its paws, just watching them.

Days later, when Dawson was capable of riding his mule, the trapper showed him the easiest trail to Ouray. Dawson left the trapper behind and rode slowly down the mountain as the wolf padded alongside.

Toward evening, Dawson heard the distinct call of another wolf in the distance. The wolf traveling beside him paused. His demeanor changed sharply. His eyes flashed, keenly alert, and his ears perked up as he looked around.

A quick glance passed between them as if they communicated their goodbyes with just a look from one to the other. Then the wolf turned toward the sound, and Dawson watched as it loped deeper into the forest, never looking back.

When Dawson got into town, people listened in awe, as he told them the story. He explained how the grizzly attacked his mule and himself, how he'd shot and stabbed the bear and believed it must've died from its wounds. He described his encounter with the injured wolf and how the giant French trapper had set his broken leg, built a shelter, and kept the fire going, saving Dawson's life. Before he'd finished the tale, a small crowd had gathered around.

The town folk were looking at him oddly, and once again asked him to describe the wolf and the trapper. They listened, but didn't exactly believe Dawson, and told him why.

Thing was, they claimed, there was only one-way down that mountain canyon. It led straight into town, and no other soul had been seen going up that mountain trail. Only Dawson and his partner had traveled into the high country recently, and Dawson was the only one to have come down it.

Then they explained that the mountain-man Dawson had just described was someone they'd known.

Legend was, the Frenchman had been the first victim of the rogue bear, believed to have been killed by it ten years ago in a blizzard similar to the one that just occurred. The grizzly had been killing miners and mountain-men ever since.

It happened in the same place Dawson said he'd been attacked.

Seems a couple of local hunters came upon the bloody camp-site and found the trapper's mules loaded with valuable furs and all his supplies. Breakfast dishes were scattered across the camp. Grizzly tracks were found all over the ground, along with a large, bear ear.

No one knew exactly what had happened to the six-foot-four mountain-man. Other than the vast amount of blood, no trace was ever found of him or his wolf-dog.

Dawson could only shake his head in disbelief because that mountain-man had saved his life. He had to be real.

Dawson slept on the floor of the little town's only tavern, beside the wood-stove until he felt well enough to travel.

When he mounted up and rode off, he still wondered who really had saved him. Dawson wished he'd asked the Frenchman's name. That wolf had looked peculiar, as if it could've been the offspring of a dog-wolf mix.

Something mysterious had happened on that mountain. He wouldn't have survived alone. He couldn't say whether it was a ghostly or heavenly spirit or just a stranger who'd gone up the mountain unnoticed. But someone had helped him.

Dawson would probably never figure that one out. He was just glad to be alive and going home.

Denise Lee Branco

Denise Lee Branco is an award-winning author and inspirational speaker who continues to believe, dream, and overcome so those who meet her recognize the possibilities within themselves.

Denise's first book, *Horse at the Corner Post: Our Divine Journey*, has not only won a silver medal in the Living Now Book Awards, but also has  touched lives and assisted various charities in raising much needed funds ever since.

Denise is a member of American Horse Publications, California Writers Club, Independent Book Publishers Association, and Northern California Publishers and Authors. She has served as Northern California Publishers and Authors vice-president and as a board member of the California Writers Club, Sacramento Branch.

Follow Denise on Twitter @DeniseLeeBranco and visit www.DeniseLeeBranco.com to learn more about her.

DENISE LEE BRANCO
Keep Moving Forward

Grieving the loss of my beloved horse, Freedom, I felt ever so driven to share our story. But how? I searched online for author groups and found Northern California Publishers and Authors (NCPA), which I now realize will always be home for me. It sparked my writing and publishing journey.

It looked like a wonderful organization to join. I remember my first NCPA meeting years ago. I stepped into the room eager but intimidated by all the incredibly talented authors and publishers. I left with new friendships. I felt inspired to tell Freedom's story. I experienced overwhelming support. It's where life as a published author began.

I dug in, consuming all I could about the literary world, the publishing industry, and business. I joined other organizations as well—some writer-publisher associations and some niche organizations. It was the best way to broaden my knowledge and make necessary connections. I weighed the good and the bad. Ultimately I decided to independently publish my first book, *Horse at the Corner Post: Our Divine Journey*. It won a silver medal in the Living Now Book Awards! What an exciting way to honor my dear horse, Freedom. I was touched. And then, my colleagues elected me vice-President of NCPA. I didn't see that one comin'! What an honor! I felt privileged!

My mission in writing and publishing *Horse at the Corner Post* was to pay tribute to my beloved horse. That meant I would share Freedom's story with everyone that I could, far and wide. I would let his spirit guide me in how to do just that—by writing. But when I finished the book, the work was not over. I'll never forget what I learned at one of my first NCPA meetings—a book does not sell itself. Authors have to get up and speak to crowds. What? Say that again. I once chose to transfer from a job because it required public speaking, and now I'm supposed to speak? Voluntarily?

I also learned that published authors often have to travel, sometimes great distances. Flying? Well, I hadn't done that one either, not in more than a decade. I had such a fear of flying since 9/11. But the passion to tell the world about my beloved Freedom was more important to me than letting my fears hold me back.

Believe me, writing, publishing, and marketing have not been easy. I often go through struggles and then "I-give-up" thoughts, followed by restored faith and reinvention. Although I have one published horse book and I have a book about other beloved pets in the making, I consider myself more of a spiritual and inspirational author than an animal storyteller or anything else. The stories that I enjoy writing most are the ones that inspire people and help them see the Divine at work.

The greatest part of this journey as an author isn't material at all. It's those written notes I've received. It's the moments with people—readers of all ages—who share how my book or just how "just being me" has inspired them. To find out that I made a difference in someone's life...wow. Now that is what I live for. That is my purpose. And guess what? These days I can't wait to get on a plane. Speaking in front of groups isn't that bad after all. I look forward to the future and creating even more inspirational presentations.

How about you? What is your yearning? Is it writing a book? Is it traveling to a place you've never been? You must take that first step of faith. I guarantee it will be scary. The venture may even feel colossal. It was for me, but take my journey as proof: you can succeed. Reach out and find a support network like I found in NCPA. If you work hard, keep moving forward no matter what, and embrace new opportunities along the way, you will find all your efforts will be rewarded. Your life will forever change. That I know for sure.

Loraine Holden

Loraine Holden has a broad background in biology and medicine. Her experience combines hands-on work with patients and studying the relationships of biochemistry and dis- ease. Her master of science degree dealt with the cytochrome enzymes.

She attended medical school at the University of Colorado for more than three years, and con-ducted research at the University of Rochester, Hahnemann University and the University of Colorado in biochemistry and physiology. She did library research and technical writing for Smith Kline and French Pharmaceutical Co. She has taught college courses in anatomy, physiology and bacteriology.

Loraine is an ardent advocate for exercise. She feels that learning physical skills produces confidence and reduces stress. She has overcome arthritis and other ailments and wants to help others gain a long and vigorous life.

LORAINE HOLDEN
Machu Picchu

At Machu Picchu I pressed my hands against the obelisk known as the Hitching Post of the Sun and felt definite pulsations. From my knowledge of anatomy, I know you can't feel your pulse in your palms. Was I being connected to a mystic energy, experiencing the famous Peruvian ruins in a unique way? My education has been in the sciences of biology and medicine. I've learned to be skeptical of phenomena that aren't verifiable using scientific instruments. I might have dismissed my strange sensations if I hadn't experienced other phenomena in the Vilcabamba Range in the days before visiting these famous ruins.

More than a million tourists come every year to see Machu Picchu. They take the train from Cuzco and then one of the crowded buses from Agua Caliente up a steep road with many switchbacks to spend a few hours at Machu Picchu. They listen to a guide, jostle with others in a group to take similar pictures. They climb some of the more than three thousand steps of the one-hundred-nine stairways to the various levels in the ruins and then relax at the snack bar, making sure not to miss their bus and train back to Cuzco.

Backpackers take a three- or four-day trek on what is called the Inca Trail. Starting from Kilometer 88, a stop on the railroad between Cuzco and Quillabamba, they hike past lesser ruins, climb three passes, and reach Machu Picchu at a higher level than the tourist buses do. More than sixty thousand hikers a year take this route, ignoring warnings of thievery in the crowded campsites.

To avoid crowds, I signed up for a 1997 trip away from civilization that included ancient trails high in the Vilcabamba Range. After seeing ruins near Cuzco and Pisac, we would ride horses, starting at the historic village of Ollantaytombo on a centuries-old trail that began at the Urubamba River. This is the river that farther along makes a *U*-shaped bend twenty-five-hundred feet below Machu Picchu. The steep cliffs above the river and jungle vegetation had made the site inaccessible to the Spaniards who conquered the rest of Peru.

Our plan was to ride horses four days in the mountains over passes up to fifteen-thousand feet high and on the fifth day join part of the Inca Trail ending at the railroad. We would take a train to Agua Caliente in time for an afternoon bus to Machu Picchu, descend, spend the night in town then take an early morning bus for another exploration of the site when crowds were thinner.

Mules would carry tents, sleeping bags, and cooking gear, but each of our group of six needed to carry our own packs with protective clothing for sun, wind, or rain. We would need a rain parka, rain pants, warm jacket and a broad-brimmed hat to deal with changeable weather throughout the day. Temperature varies greatly between sunshine and shadow. A crew of Peruvians would go ahead to prepare lunch or set up tents at each camp site, then cook meals as well as take care of the horses and mules.

Our journey up valleys across passes to other canyons and ridges of the Vilcabamba Range was an end in itself. I felt akin to the early Spaniards, exploring high, bleak mountains on horseback. Sometimes the trail went past small villages. We saw crops on centuries-old terraces. Some small, potato fields had rows going down instead of across the slopes. This was to prevent rotting of potatoes from heavier rains.

We saw horizontal trails on the steepest slopes where flocks of sheep were grazing. Centuries ago these slopes would have been used by domesticated llamas. Their split lips and softer feet were less damaging to the earth.

In a few small areas on hillsides, the eighteen-inch dry bunch grasses had been burned so the new grass would come in green and lush in the rainy season. The soil is held in place by grass roots, so no damage is done like when a rain forest is denuded by fires. I saw only dark brown earth everywhere in the mountains, unlike the bare red clay soils that are left when tropical forests are cut. As a soil scientist in Ecuador had explained on another trip, rain-forest trees have a network of filamentous fungi interlacing their roots, helping to absorb nutrients. Burning the forest to plant crops destroys these fungi. After one good crop, the denuded land soon becomes a sterile desert as nutrients are washed away by torrential rains. Here on valley land, people grow corn, beans, and quinoa (a grain containing a complete protein) as well as more potatoes. The cold, dry air allows villagers to freeze-dry potatoes for later use.

Cold, dry air had also preserved mummies buried in the fetal position in tombs. Many holes indicating looted tombs were on a steep hillside above the ruins of Pisac near Cuzco. These and the many terraced hillsides around Cuzco show how the pre-Columbian peoples were so agile. They could use areas we would call inaccessible for either graves or crops. If, indeed, most terraced land had been planted, it is no wonder that peasants needed only one-third of their crops for themselves. Another third was used by the Inca government to feed warriors and workers on the many public projects, and the rest was stored for emergencies.

Our horses responded to signals despite wearing only simple halters of braided fibers. At first I prevented my horse from stopping to eat on the way. I relented when it seemed he wanted to put some distance between himself and the next horse, so he had room to scramble quickly uphill to the next switchback.

Some of our group walked part of the time though all were good riders. One woman got a headache but no other symptoms of altitude sickness. Going to a lower altitude is the cure for liquid in the lungs, the most dangerous symptom. James, our leader, told about a trip when a heavy June snowfall panicked one person. Breathing from an oxygen tank and calm reassurances were all she needed. In fact, the storm prevented a decent. On another trip, an injured person was carried down the trail on a stretcher more quickly by running Peruvians than if put on a horse.

Having climbed thirty of the fourteen-thousand-foot peaks in Colorado, I had no fear of altitude. I expected the Andes to be similar to the Rockies. The Vilcabamba Range had slopes twice as steep. Distant snow-covered peaks like Salkantay, the Savage Mountain, looked higher and more rugged than the best of Colorado's giants. No wonder ancient peoples worshiped peaks as gods.

Our first campsite, Chanka Chuko, was at an abandoned way

station on this pre-Inca road. It was on a level area surrounded by rounded hills covered with short grasses. A small stream meandered into a pond of about a third of an acre. A tattered thatched hut near a crumbling stone wall crouched at the far end of the pond. White mists rose at dusk from a deep gorge to the south as the wind died down.

That night when going back to my tent from the latrine tent, it seemed I had to keep dodging bushes. How could that be possible? The pictures I took that afternoon were of pasture land. Then I saw that some bushes had oval leaves that gleamed like gold. I swished my walking stick in front of me but contacted nothing. The leaves just fluttered out of the way. I called out to Sandy in the tent near mine. "Look at these golden leaves that flutter when I swish my stick." She answered, "Anything that flutters is probably bats. I'm not interested."

I stayed outside and looked around. I saw silhouettes of leafless trees extending from the low hills into the night sky and the golden-leafed bushes remained. My heart started pounding as I heard panting as from a dog coming from behind and passing closely to stand about ten feet in front of me. In a low voice I asked, "Are you the spirit of coyote?" knowing it is a special animal for North American Indians. Soon I heard the panting going toward the pond but saw nothing.

Next morning I asked our leader if this had been a holy place. He didn't think so and said, "There are no coyotes in South America, only a small fox that doesn't live around here." How can I explain my weird experiences? Had a scene from past ages entered my consciousness? Was timberline higher then? At latitudes near the equator maybe trees could grow at thirteen thousand feet. In Colorado at about forty degrees north latitude, the timberline is eleven thousand feet. Had trees been cut down in the Andes like they had been in Turkey and Greece centuries ago? Had trees been used as rollers to haul giant stones for temples? Even before the Spaniards, had locals altered the ecology?

At our second campsite, Ancascocha, at thirteen thousand, seven-hundred feet, pink and gray layers of an uplifted former sea floor of sandstone and limestone loomed above us. The slope on the other side of camp dropped precipitously to a jade green lake, fed by rivulets from snow on granite crags. As we entered our camp, two children rounded up their sheep and disappeared over a low hill.

That night I sat on a rock above the camp. Here I saw smaller ethereal silver leaves on a network of small twigs that floated away in the breeze. More amazing was a series of images on the back of one of the tents, lighted from within so the occupant could read. First I saw a bear half-hiding behind a pine tree. Wind shook the tent, and a giant dragonfly spread its wings on the slanting trunk of a tree fern. Then I saw images of two small creatures crawling up on the right. Before I could see if they were lizards or weasels, the scene changed to a desolate white expanse with a charred trunk in an icy lake. Later a scene in ochre and reddish brown looked like a ruined village. The show was over when the person in the tent turned off his light.

Next day, on an alternate trail, after surmounting a thirteen-thousand, eight-hundred-foot pass and contouring down we looked over a steep canyon to see the third campsite at thirteen-thousand, two-hundred feet. The name Yawar Maquii, meaning Hand of Blood, even sounded ominous. I felt even more like an explorer braving the unknown. Boulders up to twelve feet in diameter must have broken off from the cliff above and tumbled down to two sandy flat areas. Most had landed to the right of our tents. A small stream went through camp to plunge several hundred feet down to the left. Here we saw no evidence of sheep or other horses. What a place to spend Halloween! The others had their martinis, and I drank plain Vermouth. After showing makeshift costumes and telling stories, we went directly to bed to get out of the cold.

Sometime in the night I was awakened by a low reverberation. Could it be from an avalanche starting hundreds of feet above? I crawled out of my tent to look at the mountains and the sky. I sighed with relief when I saw distant lightning and figured the rumblings had been thunder. A single, high-pitched noise like a scream made me bury myself in my sleeping bag.

I couldn't sleep, wondering why this place was called the Hand of Blood. Before the Spaniards, the Inca let many isolated tribes keep customs like human sacrifice to mountain gods to get rain. Freeze-dried mummies of little girls wrapped in rich textiles along with ceremonial objects have been found near ruins on high mountains. Their chests had not been cut to remove the heart like Mayan priests did. Some showed blows to the head. Others might have been drugged and left to die. The Incas, rulers of a Quechua speaking tribe from Lake Titicaca, claimed to be sons of the sun. After conquering a large territory—bigger than the Roman empire—they introduced sun worship. Inca temples were lower, and only lamas were sacrificed.

Our fourth campsite Pocarcancha was much lower, near an archaeologic site being excavated and restored. It wasn't a true temple though it did have a u-shaped wall around an existing boulder. It might have been used for other celebrations. Our leader had pointed out features of previous ruins to look for when we got to Machu Picchu. Ruins near Cuzco, Pisac, and Ollantaytambo built by ancient tribes had giant well-fitting stones to which the Incas had added smaller stones. Machu Picchu is an example of grand imperial Inca architecture built in the ninety years before the Spaniards arrived in Peru about 1530.

The fifth camp was across from the railroad tracks where a small village caters to hikers of the Inca Trail. That night our leader said, "Explore Machu Picchu the next two days at your own pace." He told us some of the features to look for until we had to run to our tents to listen to a deluge of rain that lasted all night. The storm god Illapa was showing his power.

The next afternoon at Machu Picchu I started by climbing many stone steps to the highest watchtower. Nearby was one of the special stones, the horizontal Funerary Rock, shaped like a big couch. I descended to the main temple area. A large sacred hunk of the underlying bedrock is enclosed by a horse-shoe shaped wall. Signs and barriers prevent tourists from touching this rock. Several fountain falls descend into a series of ceremonial baths. In the main courtyard of the temple, some horizontal stones about one by two feet, shaped and polished for the ceremonial sacrifice of llamas, face a narrow altar.

I went up more stone steps to another special rock, the Intihuatana, the Hitching Post of the Sun. This polished obelisk had been set at a precise angle to indicate the solstices. Nothing prevented touching it, so I placed my hands on the surface. I felt definite pulsations. It wasn't my pulse, so I must have felt mystic energy.

I descended to a path to the east where on a grassy plaza I

saw a flat slab of rock about ten by thirty feet that had been set on edge. This rock just before the entrance to the trail to the Temple of the Moon up the hill called the Huayna Picchu. I couldn't go up because the trail was closed after a recent fire. It was getting late, so I went back to catch the last bus going down.

My seat mate was a New Age adherent. He said his group came for the spiritual energy here. This conversation came after we spent days at ruins in the Sacred Valley of the Urubamba River to get in tune with the Ancients before going to Machu Picchu. He explained how to integrate the power of the special rocks. "First start at the Death Rock and imagine lying on it and going to the underworld as the sun does at night. Become purified as you walk through the temple area then climb to the Intihuatana. Touch it to receive its power. Descend to the big rock on edge. Touch it to return most of this energy back to the earth, the Pachamamma." I wondered if these activities might be related to practices of the Inca religion or those of ancient tribes. Still this simple ritual could give meaning to this mythic place.

After a relaxing dinner and sleeping in a real bed, we were eager to return to the ruins the next morning on the first bus. It would be a chance to take pictures without a lot of tourists in them. Our leader said to look for details like holes drilled in the stone of doorways. Had they secured a wooden door or a braided rope indicating no admittance? Even now when a peasant leaves his house, he puts a stick across the doorway, knowing that, by custom, no one will enter.

I wanted to return to the Intihuatana, hoping to be alone. However, I saw a New Age group standing around it. With joined hands and bowed heads, they listened to affirmations from their leader. They were more in tune with the spirit of the place than the tourists I saw the day before who climbed over a rope to have their pictures taken.

We don't know why Machu Picchu was built. With its many agricultural terraces and good water supply, it was a self-contained city but not a fortress. Since most of the unearthed skeletons were female, it might have been a holy place served by chosen women. The pottery there is from the Inca period not from the Chauvin that extended from 1000 B.C. to 100 A.D. It wasn't made by Nazca or other tribes conquered by the Inca. The site was probably abandoned about 1570 and only discovered in 1911 by American historian Hiram Bingham.

We may never have answers, but mystery makes the site more intriguing. I'm glad I saw it as the culmination of our journey over the Vilcabamba Range. Feeling the power and majesty of the Andes for five days in sun, wind, and rain put me in touch with the forces of nature and the Apu or power of mountains. I wonder if my paranormal experiences were a signal not to rely wholly on science but be open to spirituality. However, I tried but failed to connect to an alternate universe with a shaman in a remote village on a tributary of the Amazon in 2013. A better goal might be to help preserve natural and primitive places and, thus, revere Mother Earth, the Pachamamma.

Thea Holmdahl

Thea Holmdahl was educated in Hannover Germany, where she graduated from the Handelsschule Buhman, a business college, with a degree of secretarial stenographer. She worked as legal secretary both in Germany as well as in San Jose, California. Thea attained her bachelor's degree from California State University, Sacramento, with a major in philosophy and minor in history.

For a number of years she worked in the California State Legislature. She is an alumnus of the CSSAA. She took writing instructions in an autobiography class offered at Sierra College in Roseville, California, for several years.

She is a member of the Suburban Writers Club and Northern California Publishers & Authors,. She also belongs to the Hermann Sohne at the German Turnverein, located in Sacramento, California.

THEA HOLMDAHL
I Was There

I was there when the wall came down—the Berlin Wall and its extension which divided Germany from north to south. Erected in September of 1961, the wall kept people from entering the DDR, so they wanted us to believe.

The "DDR" was the name for this eastern part of Germany from the time of occupation by the Soviet victors at the end of WW II in May of 1945. The acronym stands for *Deutsche Demokratische Republik*, translated to mean German Democratic Republic. At the time of capitulation, Germany had been divided into four sectors, the English, American, and French in the West and the Soviet sector in the East. This eastern border from that time on remained heavily guarded.

It kept families apart and people from traveling freely East to West or visa versa. Soon refugees would cross the border to find better living conditions in the West. They had to do so in secret under great peril. But the trend increased so much the DDR erected a deterrent in the form of a twelve-foot wall. In some places it extended nine feet deep.

My family escorted me across that border a short while after I had, in 1987, resettled in Hannover, my hometown. We traveled by car that ninety-mile corridor to Berlin. We were held up in three-hour-long lines waiting for East German citizens in Soviet uniforms to process our passports, traveling permits, and money exchange in arduous fashion. These border officials, who gave us a rather frosty reception in handling our papers, seemed foreign to us. Their frown appeared hostile. They made no eye contact, and they did not speak to us. We felt we could be arrested at any moment and for whatever reason. They might have been Soviet spies for all we knew.

Our first stop behind the border was a dimly lit warehouse; we could buy vodka and household goods at reduced prices, we were told. We found little to interest us, so we drove on into the west sector of Berlin.

This was June of 1989, about forty-four years after war's end, yet the environment gave the impression that time had passed it by. Little reconstruction could be seen. The rubble of war had been removed, yet nothing of distinction had replaced it. We saw rows of standardized, concrete high-rises where the Germans lived without noticeable comfort, nor even vegetation for beautification. No sidewalks accompanied the street, just lanes worn into the earth by foot-traffic, leading around water puddles created incidentally, not by design.

Eventually, we found a little restaurant which might have once been a private residence. They served asparagus soup for a late luncheon. However, the line was so long we doubted they would have enough to serve us at the end. But they did, and it tasted good.

Further down the street we encountered the *Gedaechtnis Kirche*, the church left destroyed in remembrance of the bombing raids on Berlin in the 1940s. We walked on along the Tiergarten Strasse, a wide avenue in a park-like setting. Then we stopped at a Russian war memorial to watch uniformed soldiers ceremoniously marching in stilted goose-step back and forth. We lingered a while. The exercise seemed puffed-up bravado, we agreed, its meaning having faded with the passage of time—a message lost on the younger generation.

We continued along the Tiergarten Strasse to the Brandenburg Gate. On the top the Quadriga statue, the four-horse chariot faced east when it should have been facing west, an observer said. The conquerors made their point.

The gate itself, of course, was blocked by a twelve-foot wall, but the erection of a large platform allowed observers to look over the wall into East Berlin. We climbed up for the view. It seemed bleak and gray over there. In disbelief, we saw for ourselves the uniformed East Germans patrolling the ground with shouldered rifles, ready to shoot at anyone, even their own countrymen who dared to escape over that wall. By all accounts, it seemed clear that they had been indoctrinated, all too willing to follow orders. They had to see it as a treasonous affront to their communist government when someone wanted to leave. For the Westerners, the view portrayed a twisted reality; we found it hard to understand how citizens of a conquered nation could be restrained for so many years after the war.

"How could there come a change?" I wondered "A change *must* come," I thought. I had lived in California for twenty-seven years and become an American citizen, but long before as a child, I lived all though World War II in the nearby city of Hannover. And then in 1987, while still packing my things to revisit my native Germany, I heard news reports of those now-famous words spoken by President Ronald Reagan: "Mr. Gorbachev, tear down that wall!" And to me then, at that very moment, so close to that infamous wall, those seemed to be the only sane words that existed in the world.

We walked on to the nearby *Reichstag* and to Hitler's former Chancellery. Nothing much remained of the infamous dictator's dream of grandeur—only the rubble of bricks and mortar, symbolic of work done by Hitlers architect, Albert Speer, a short time before the capitulation. He lived to write about it in his book, *Memoirs Inside the Third Reich*, a story which made the scene before me more meaningful.

Next we searched for the famous street called *Kurfuersten Damm* to recapture the former chic of restaurants and shopping centers. But we could not find it. We asked a passerby where we might find something close to it. However, he had no clue what we meant. He explained he was from East Germany, near the city of Dresden. He was in a hurry, looking for a last-minute present for his wife before he had to find his way back across the border. His visiting day visa would expire in a short while (they were issued a visa to the West only a few times a year).

We asked him, "How are things in the East?"

"Very bad," he answered. "We have nothing, not even lumber or a nail to repair a roof, nor mortar or paint to refinish a house." He reported on similar shortages ever since the end of the war in 1945. "Nothing is issued to us by the present government administration. We are in bad shape and don't know how improvements can come about in our so-called planned economy. Things are falling apart everywhere."

He was a young man, perhaps in his early forties, and at an age that he could hardly have known how things had been before the occupation. He seemed desperate. We could feel his dilemma. I heard what he said and understood his anxiety. I don't know why, but I touched his shoulder and said with certainty from my heart, "This will not last. It is not natural, and a change will come soon."

He looked at me with doubtful eyes and replied, "I hope so, but I don't believe it." He dropped his faint smile and looked sadly at the floor in front of his feet. Soon we parted, waiving a cordial goodbye.

To this day I am wondering how I could have said those words with such certainty to a perfect stranger. Where did that faith come from? I had no knowledge of a change. However, I had a sense of something different in the air. Nothing had been in the news recently that would give me confidence of future changes.

I remember a time, however, when there had been talk. I overheard it when I was vacationing in Mallorca a few months before this encounter. We visited a fashionable town square in El Arenal, where we enjoyed live music and danced to the popular tunes. Different nationalities had congregated, and we seemed to hear conversations of changes coming. Nothing in particular, only disbelief at the continued situation of East Germans forced to live closed-in behind a wall in modern times. No plots. No plans. No solutions. Nothing concrete, just a pervasive sense that it could not remain this way.

I had forgotten that chatter, but it came to mind a few months later when I heard news that thousands of refugees from East Germany had escaped over the Hungarian Border into Austria. And then more refugees traveled from Prague to West Germany in special trains. East Germany had closed its borders with Czechoslovakia. Then there were riots in the East German city of Dresden and mass demonstrations in the cities of Leipzig and East Berlin. They were non-violent, but the people would shout, *"Wir sind das Volk,"* meaning, "We are the people." Their shouts brought notice to their oppressive government: "*We* are the ones that count. *We* want freedom to travel, freedom of the press, and free elections."

All the rights denied for years, for their return they called.

Finally at last, there changes came to Central Committee of the Communist Party. A parliament was to form a new government; new travel laws were being drafted. East Germans would be allowed to visit to West Germany without special clearances. Thousands of East Berliners flooded to West Berlin through the notorious Checkpoint Charlie and other border crossings. The entire city celebrated the opening of the Wall.

That was the evening of November 9,1989. I remember it well. I was in Hannover, on my way to my sister's house for dinner. News came that the Berlin Wall had been opened. It was a dark night. I listened to the car radio and could not believe my ears. Reporters were shouting words of joy over the wires, celebrating with the happy crowd down in the streets of Berlin. I had lost my way and had to stop at a gas station for directions. When I told the attendants of what I had heard on the radio, they looked at me in disbelief. But they tuned in and heard the reports as well, shaking their heads while they listened.

I surprised my sister and her family with the news. They had not watched until then. We turned on the television to see young men climbing the wall. Their Champaign bottles gushed with foam. Everywhere folks danced for joy. Clearly most people in Berlin had come out to celebrate. The celebration went on for weeks while the government heads debated. However, they eventually tore the wall down for good, bit by bit, around New Year's 1990. When enterprising people began selling pieces of the wall to anyone who would pay a good price, the East Germans protested, claiming that it was *their* wall and only they could sell it. Nobody listened!

Almost the next day, people started coming to cities outside of Berlin. They came by train with the two hundred in West German currency each had received at the border to spend on goods in the West. We saw them looking into shop windows for hours, but seldom did anyone venture in to buy anything. It was all too grand and too shiny. They looked bedazzled by the oversupply, they told us later. They liked fresh fruits, like oranges and bananas. Most would stand in lines until the supply was exhausted. They had not seen them for years. Their government would not supply the markets with such expensive foreign goods.

Some of the people feared they would miss the return train

and remained reluctant to stay the night even though they were offered free beds at the railroad station or other hostelries. Such sudden new freedom was troublesome for most, and they would not trust our generosity.

Some even came by "Trabi," their government allotted car, a slow, noisy, smelly mobile running by a two-stroke engine, called *Trabant*, for which they had to wait ten years. They loved their little car, my cousin Hildegard told me. She and her husband would take little trips into the countryside and cherished each outing even though it was slow going and not without peril because the *Trabant* was unreliable. It broke down frequently, they said. And the body was actually made of carton, similar to Masonite, with a heavy coat of paint so it would not melt in the rain. It later became a collector's item.

One afternoon, soon after the borders had opened, my family and I went to the nearby town of *Braunschweig*, about fifty kilometers east of *Hannover*. We wanted to see for ourselves the Germans who had been under siege for forty-four years. Could they still be German or had communism changed them beyond recognition? A new generation had emerged that had never known anything else but a government with socialist laws and limitations.

Yes, we met them, and they were different. They were shy and did not talk unless spoken to. They voiced their opinion only reluctantly. Even when we invited them to a restaurant for coffee and cakes, they sat huddled together, hesitant to answer our questions about how life had been for them after the war had ended. We had meant it to be a celebration and a welcome; we were so glad to have them back, but they understood neither our concern, nor our curiosity, let alone our friendship. We felt a general misunderstanding of what was happening, and we realized it, but were not sure exactly how things looked so different on the other side of the fence.

We asked what had made them decide to demonstrate—at long last, and received a satisfying answer.

"We simply decided not to be afraid any longer!" they said.

Catherine Byron

Catherine Byron, a lifelong Montana resident, earned her first accolades for writing as an eighth-grader. An engraved, silver pitcher presented by Prime Minister Nehru, the first prize for an international writing contest, stands as evidence of her early passion for writing. A descendant of two generations of homesteaders, she is actively involved in managing a Montana ranch. Her love

 of the land and the people, as well as an understanding of the challenges facing the small landowner, make her a voice of the common man. Visit her webstite at www.ByronsCorner.com.

Falling heir to family papers, journals and letters dating back to the 1800s, Byron's current writing is focuses on stories from a frontier era. She gives this background for her story, *The Storm*:

Fourteen-year-old Mary Lynch arrived on Rosebud Creek, eastern Montana, from County Cavan, Ireland, in 1883, the oldest daughter in a family of eight. Her parents homesteaded a stone's throw away from the Northern Cheyenne Reservation and Tongue River Agency-Camp Merritt at Lame Deer.

In her late teens, Mary worked as a seamstress and teacher helping the Ursuline nuns with the Indian students attending St. Labre's Mission at Ashland, Montana. It was there that she met John Mahoney, a young carpenter building the Mission's first frame church. They married after a short courtship. In November of 1899, John died from surgical erysipelas after doctors removed a tumor from his neck. Mary gave birth to the couple's sixth living child two-and-a-half months after John's death.

The young widow and her six children continued to live in the couple's homestead shack until Mary filed on her own homestead in the 1920s. She worked as a laundress for the officers and soldiers stationed at Camp Merritt to provide for her family.

Summer Saturdays were a cause for celebration. It was then that 32-year-old Mary hitched the Percheron-Morgan-cross team to a wagon loaded with camping gear, a trunk filled with church clothes, and six children ages five months to ten years, and began the 25-mile trek to Sunday Mass at St. Labre's Mission.

The story of one of those trips was recounted by her second daughter, Katie, in notes and recollections of her childhood when she was in her late 70s. Katie was eight years old at the time of a great storm in July of 1900.

CATHERINE BYRON
The Storm

T here it is!" the two little kids, four-year-old Rose and two-
year-old Maurice, shouted in excitement when the familiar campsite came into view. The evening coolness rose
from the river and engulfed us, a welcome reprieve from the day's
squelching heat.

Mama unhitched and picketed the team in a shady grove of
cottonwoods on the banks of the Tongue River. With renewed energy, we climbed the giant cottonwood trees and created imaginary
forts. The warm river water was low in late July as it rippled toward
the mighty Yellowstone. Under Mama's watchful eye, we waded
near the edges catching polliwogs and minnows.

While we played, Mama spread her bright red-and-white
checkered tablecloth on the grass and set it as if it were a table for
our picnic supper. Cold, fried chicken and wild-plum-jam sand-
wiches made with Mama's fluffy homemade bread tasted so good.
It had been a long time since lunch.

After clearing the picnic, Mama sat on the wagon tongue
and nursed Baby Tot while we played one last game of tag. The
swish of the nighthawks darting and diving into clouds of mos-
quitoes and the evening chorus of crickets and frogs signaled the
approaching darkness.

The chilly night air pushed us to hurry as we rolled out the
bedrolls in the wagon box. The sleeping quarters were tight. Mama
shared her bed with Baby Tot, Maurice, and Rosie. Madge, ten
years old, Johnnie, six years old, and I, eight years old—the "big"

kids—squeezed into the other. After some jostling, we nestled between clean sheets and soft soogans—quilts—beneath the clear night sky. Mama led the night prayers, and Maurice proudly ended with his chirpy "amen."

Abruptly Johnnie thrust his arm into the air pointing at the stars. "There's the Big Dipper."

"Yes," Mama said, "and right over there is the Little Dipper." She paused, took Johnnie's hand and traced an imaginary line. "And there is Orion, the hunter."

"Which star is Papa, Mama?" Rosie's question took us all by surprise. "You said he went to heaven. Which star is he?"

"Rosie, he's the brightest one you can see up there. And his star just might be winking as he sends down hugs to each of you." Mama paused. "Let's find the brightest one." We went to sleep that night looking for the brightest star, certain it would be our papa in heaven.

The warmth of a bright, morning sun woke us early and promised another hot day. Mama nursed the baby while Madge and I opened the trunk and took out our beautifully ironed Sunday best: fresh drawers, chemises, and dresses with wide ribbon-decorated yokes and skirts with gathers that started at the neckline. Next came the little boys' blousy white shirts and knickers. We all wore dark stockings held in place by garters above our knees. Madge dampened a cloth and wiped the dust from the little boys' shoes.

Mama handed Baby Tot to Madge. "Dress him in the new rompers while Katie helps me harness the team. We need to get to the church in time for confession."

Stamping their feet and fluttering their nostrils, the horses were ready to move. Standing on the feed bucket, I helped Mama lift the heavy harness onto their wide backs. Before we hitched them to the wagon, I held the lines while she dressed in a long, black, flowing skirt with a bodice that buttoned up the front.

Making one last inspection to ensure we were fit for church, Mama licked her fingers and wiped down rooster tails in the little boys' hair. She tied my hair back with a ribbon, then stepped up onto the wagon seat, reached down for baby Tot, and watched while Madge and I helped the little kids into the wagon box. When everyone was seated, she flicked the lines. "Giddy up."

One short half-mile and we would see the white Mission church that Papa built. After Papa had finished it, he became the boss farmer for the Mission. Mama sewed and cooked for the nuns and the students there. That's where Mama and Papa met and fell in love.

The Ursuline nuns always invited us to breakfast after Mass. We looked forward to eating in their big kitchen with all the wonderful plates and cups and glasses. The food was good, too. We were their favorites, mostly because the nuns knew our parents before they married. Oh, how I looked forward to the double kiss and warm handgrip they gave us!

Sister Gertrude, cheeks flushed, scurried around the kitchen, frying bacon and eggs and brewing a tall pot of coffee. She sliced mounds of fresh-baked bread to go with the meal. She was the cook, the baker, and the doctor. Mother Thecla was Superior. Everyone visited and laughed as the smells of breakfast filled the room. The nuns asked Mama all about how we were getting along without Papa. He had been dead for eight months now. Over and over they would say, "Oh, Mary dear..."

After breakfast, Mama let us play with some of the Cheyenne kids that lived at the Mission. We studied for First Communion together, and they became our good friends. Mama helped with breakfast dishes and cleanup and visited with the nuns.

It was mid-afternoon when we left the Mission for home. The team faced into the sun as we took the trail back to Lame Deer and our homestead shack. A bank of black clouds kept growing in the west. Mama watched it but said nothing as she flicked the lines to encourage the team to walk faster. The little kids fell asleep, tired from all the excitement. Madge and I peeked into a paper bag with holes poked in it to watch the tiny yellow canary one of the girls at the Mission had given me. I couldn't wait to get home to build it a cage. The plans raced through my brain: cut some of the smaller willows down by the creek and weave them in and out.

Mama looked hard at the black clouds as we pulled into Lame Deer. "Whoa!" She brought the team to a halt outside Mr. Watters' store. He was watching the storm clouds, too. As she started to leave, he said, "Woman, you are welcome to stay here in the store until it passes."

"Thank you, Mr. Watters," Mama said. "We need to get home."

A small group of Indians pointed to the storm clouds. She nodded her head to say thank-you, but she was determined to get home.

When we were one-and-a-half miles from the store, the wind hit. Mama tied the lines, swung herself down into the wagon box, and jerked ropes off the bedrolls. Her frantic, strong tugs pulled out the soogans. One. Two. Three. Four. She gripped one by two corners and flapped it, allowing the wind to unfold and spread it before she dropped it on the floor of the wagon box. With her eyes glued on the angry clouds, she yelled, "Get down!" We scurried onto the soft cushion. Madge cradled Baby Tot, and I protected my canary. Rosie, Johnnie, and Maurice crowded in between us. Grabbing two more soogans, Mama shook them out over us like a tent. We couldn't see, but we heard her flip the heavy, big tarp over all of it, trying to make a water-repellent roof.

First we heard heavy rain—big raindrops—driven by the wind. Then hailstones as big as hen eggs pounded down. We felt them, but they didn't hurt through all the layers of padding. The team began to prance, then bolted and ran. Baby Tot sensed the danger and began to cry. "Hold him, Madge. I've got to turn the team!"

Mama clambered onto the wagon seat through the soaking rain and pounding hail. She pulled the lines hard to curb the panicky pair of blacks. "Eeeasy, now. Eeeasy, now. Eeeeeeeeasy." Her voice and firm hand on the lines calmed the trembling horses. We felt the wagon slow, turn, then begin to circle back as Mama faced the horses into the storm. "Holy Mary, Mother of God..." We heard her prayers above the howling wind.

Baby Tot belted out screams. Mama tied the lines after the horses settled and crawled back under the tarp with us. Soaking wet and cold, she pulled a soogan around herself and the baby. She opened her dress, and he nursed. "There, there, little Tot. It's okay. Mama's here." She rocked back and forth as she spoke. The sound of her voice brought calm to each of us.

Then a dull thud jarred us. A huge hailstone hit Tot's tiny head near the soft spot. Despite the soogan and the tarp layers to buffer the blow, he quit nursing, quivered, and stiffened. Mama cried out, "God, help us all." She hugged his tiny limp body and prayed, "Our Father, who art in heaven..." She hadn't yet finished the prayer when Tot started to cry. It was dark under the soogans and tarp, but it sounded like Mama was sobbing when she whispered,

"Thank you, Lord."

At last the wind died down, and the rain quit. We were all soaked and cold. Water had poured into the wagon box through every crack and had gushed in when Mama moved the tarp to go out and settle the team. Mama peeled back the wet tarp and lifted the soggy soogans, then checked each one of us. No bruises. We were all shivering, and our drenched, church clothes dripped water onto our shoes. But the storm was over, and we were unharmed.

When Mama took her bearings to figure out where we were, she spied an occupied Indian shack. "Let's pay them a visit." She led the way as we walked toward the make-shift house through ankle-deep water and grinding hailstones. I shuddered with every step.

The Indians saw us coming. The buck came toward us dressed in white man's clothing. He asked in Cheyenne, "What are you doing here?" It was Mockey Bock, a.k.a. Big Back. He had served as an Indian Scout at Fort Keogh during the uprisings. A tall, friendly, and humorous old fellow, his round face carried a big grin framed by two braids about a foot long. He spoke broken English.

"We are on our way home from Mass at the Mission, Mockey Bock—" Mama didn't have to explain any further.

"Ameonie, come in." He used Mama's Cheyenne name. It meant "Great White Walking Woman." The Northern Cheyenne people knew and loved our mother. She often walked to deliver babies and visit the sick, sometimes long distances. She treated little Indian kids' sores with a special ointment. Their people had so much scrofula—a form of tuberculosis—running sores, and scabs on the face. She made sure that we kids didn't come into contact with anything touched by the ones with these sores.

Mama accepted Mockey Bock's invitation, and we went into his dirt-floored shack. Squaw Cora was blind in one eye. A stick had flown up and put her eye out when she was chopping wood for a fire many years before. She was very clean considering her primitive conditions.

Bunk-bed boards nailed to the wall with two legs on the outside formed a bed box filled with straw or hay. The two blankets on the bed were noticeably dirty and worn. Squaw Cora busied herself making supper and coffee using the only stove they had: a small pile of wood cinders glowing red in the middle of the floor. The vent for the smoke was a half-sash window nearby. Her matches were flint-rock sparks.

Cora was careful to wash her hands before cooking. She mixed a bread-like biscuit dough using a little baking powder, salt, no shortening, flour and water and worked it with her hands. She flattened it into circles about quarter-inch thick. She arranged the glowing coals to hold the heat before gently laying the dough patties on them. When turned, they were golden brown. A few black ashes could be dusted off when we ate them. I took many a bite when I was a kid. They were similar to Mama's biscuits but were different from anything we got at home. I can still hear how they sizzled while they baked!

We drank coffee and ate the bread. Cora served us ripe chokecherries that she had prepared by crushing them into mush, adding a little flour and pounding them on a rock with a rock. Then she put them on a rag where they dried in a thick layer that she cut like fudge.

Next she gave us jerked beef—maybe it was dog meat—with the coal-baked biscuits. The jerky was sliced thin, in sheet-like pieces and hung over a bower to dry. A bower was a make-shift porch covered with boughs for shade that always had a pole for hanging meat to dry. The hot sun toughened and hardened the exposed surface, flies or no flies. If the flies found a damp and juicy spot, they deposited eggs, and maggots hatched. The maggots were simply scratched off, and the meat was used. Jerky was usually eaten raw.

They sprinkled the dirt floor of their little shack with water carried from the creek, and it was scraped smooth by their moccasins. Only a few Cheyenne had log houses. Most lived in tents and tepees that they had banked against the cold by shoveling dirt along the lower edge.

One old Indian and his squaw, Hotoa-gus (Old Bull Sheep), came to Mockey Bock's shack to see us in our soggy state. In wonder, they said Almighty God looked after Ameonie. They told her she walked on water.

After the storm passed and we climbed out of the wagon, I discovered that my canary died. Maybe it had been hit by a hailstone, or maybe someone had crowded it too tight. After supper, Madge and I stood outside the shack and cried looking at the tiny dead bird. Mockey Bock heard the fuss and came out to comfort us. He pointed to a tree fork and made the signs and said, "*Enuits,* dead," meaning, "It's dead." We nodded in agreement. He thought for a bit then asked, "Do you want to lay it to rest in the trees like the Cheyenne lay the dead away? Wrap it in a rag?" We listened.

Mockey Bock took several steps away, bent down, and showed us a spot where we could bury it like a white man. He went into the shack and got the knife from Cora. The women prepared all the hides and cut all the meat, so they always carried the knife. He sat on the ground tailor-fashion and dug the canary's grave, putting a kind hand on it before we covered it.

Before dark, Mama checked to see if we could drive the team the five remaining miles to our homestead shack. But the water was still too high to venture across Lame Deer Creek. The runoff from the storm had turned it from a trickle to a torrent as it roared toward Rosebud Creek on its way to the Yellowstone. The sun had dropped behind the Wolf Mountains, and soon it would be dark. The horses had quit trembling, but Mama didn't want to try to unharness them. It was best to let them rest undisturbed, she said.

Cora and Mockey Bock gave us their bed that night. They slept on the floor so that Ameonie's little flock could rest well. All six of us slept crosswise in the bunk, and Mama slept in a chair with her head resting on the bed. Baby Tot slept at the end nearest her. She rested one hand on his chubby little leg most of the night, and her other hand worked the wooden rosary beads.

At first light in the morning, we reorganized the camp gear in the wagon. We rolled the soggy soogans inside the tarps and used them as seats for the short ride home. Before we left, Mockey Bock asked little Johnnie, "Your Mama got any woman chicken?" He knew that if he asked a child for something, he would often get it! "Mmmmmmmmmm! Papa?"

Mama smiled and said, "Thank you, Mockey Bock and Cora! We will see what we can do about the chickens."

On our way home that morning, we could see what a terrible storm it had been. All the grass and weeds had been mowed to the ground. Hailstones had peeled the sagebrush and left egg-sized pock marks in the mud. Mud balls, sticks, and brush had washed down the coulee. Rocks—mostly volcanic clinker and shale—had been shoved long distances. The raging water had washed dead birds into the barbs of the fences. I had never seen the rain come so fast in so short a time.

It was almost noon by the time we got home. Mama and I unhitched the wagon then took the team to the barn for some oats while we removed the wet harnesses. The horses rolled and rolled after we turned them loose. They were as glad as we were to be home.

"Well, we'd better hang the soogans to dry," Mama said. With that, we started unloading our camping outfit and doing chores.

Mama made sure that little Johnnie delivered a hen and rooster to Mockey Bock and Cora within the week. It was hard to tell who was most pleased because all three of them had big smiles. Mockey Bock and Cora had become our good friends.

Daniel Babka

D aniel Babka grew up in a small town in the middle of America. He served in VISTA (the domestic Peace Corps), attended law school, and studied at a theological seminary.

He has worked as a community organizer and managed housing in New York City's toughest neighborhoods. More recently, Daniel ran two small, start-up companies. His novel, *No More Illusions,* was described by  Kirkus Reviews as "accomplished, ambitious crime fiction…a multilayered tale that has shades of California noir à la Chinatown."

Lightning Strikes, his coming-of-age novella set in 1959, has also received glowing reviews.

DANIEL BABKA

Two States
and a Thousand Miles

Most days my dad carried a moneybag and a blackjack for his trip to the bank, not a briefcase like people do now. He was never around much except for vacations and boating weekends on Lake Erie. People trusted him to cash their payroll checks at the family's tavern, and he let them run a tab when their money ran short. Seemed to me, when I think about him now, he always had a cigar in the corner of his mouth and was busy with the business.

My dad took pride when I became the first kid in the family to go to college, even though I had to take one of those remedial math classes. Journalism and the law are what interested me. Like most people I wasn't paying attention to the war back then. Woodward and Bernstein hadn't hit the front pages yet.

My dad bought a big white, 1962 Chrysler Imperial LeBaron the year before he moved the family to Florida. I stayed behind to finish my senior year in high school. The Imperial was the same make Omar Sharif and the Duke and Duchess of Windsor drove—three-hundred-forty horsepower, red-gunsight taillights, and burgundy leather seats. It sat in the driveway next to my grandparents' lilac tree for months, tempting me.

A friend and I pushed it out to the main road around midnight. We both looked at each other and smiled when I turned the key. The motor purred. Fifty yards from the end of the quarter-mile run, I edged past a Ford coupe with four on the floor before the Imperial went into a skid and plowed into a snow bank. Ice packed around the engine block, but there wasn't a scratch on—the car thank God. After that, my dad left the Chrysler in Florida for my mom to use. He drove a thin, metal, silver, two-door Plymouth back and forth to check on the business and make sure my grandparents kept me in line.

When the semester started, Dad dropped me off on campus. Later that day, he put his arm out the window and waved good-bye as he rounded the corner. The small compact pinged harmlessly as he shifted gears. I watched the tail lights fast-forward to the next block before they faded from view. He was headed back to Florida where he'd bought a home with a concrete driveway and a canal in the back. I guessed the land developers thought those places would be perfect for snowbirds like him from the Midwest who were starved for sunshine and wanted shiny new lives.

* * *

Two days later and two states away, at 12:30 Tuesday morning, a man named C. K. (Tick) Sheldon walked out of a bar with a half-case of beer under his belt. He climbed into his car, drove three miles down the road, and crossed the centerline. My dad's Plymouth was coming from the opposite direction. Tick drove those headlights straight into the Plymouth's motor. The steering wheel smashed against my dad's chest. He was dead in an instant, along with the time together we'd begun to enjoy. Even now, I can close my eyes and see my aunt and uncle at the bottom of the rooming-house stairs the morning they told me. The simple peering way each of their souls reached out touched me deeply.

I threw myself into my studies after that. I suppose I did become more solitary, if not by design, then propelled by chance. For a while nothing seemed to matter. His death changed me in ways I didn't understand, extending far beyond my first marriage. Decades passed.

* * *

Four years after my divorce, I fell in love with Sarah. When we visited Tahoe and she told me it was over between us, I felt like an air mattress slowly being decompressed. I hadn't seen it coming. I felt empty, the same way I did when I realized my father was never coming back.

I didn't accept either one of these two events as final. I thought they were illusions that would give way to a resurrection of our meeting once again—that things would take a different turn. I've always been an incurable romantic. Or maybe it's simply because I've always had a hard time accepting reality when it startles me.

So I went about my life injured by an unrecognized fear of abandonment that colored who I was. I thought about swimming too far from shore when I was in my forties in Delaware on a business trip. Later, when another relationship ended, I considered swimming across the lake near where I lived and what I would do when I reached the point where either shore seemed just out of reach. Would I panic, give up, or find the strength to push on? I sat in my car and saw only gray. I never walked to the edge of the water, even though I ached for the test.

I used to have a recurring dream that my father wasn't dead. At some point, I expected he'd walk back into my life or I'd find him in a small town when I was driving cross-country. He'd unexpectedly find himself torn between two worlds—the same way I did. But I'm older now. Adversity doesn't seem so personal anymore.

* * *

I walked along the rim trail at dusk that night. A woman emerged from the shadows and climbed over the rail on the bridge that spanned the canyon and the river coursing beneath us. A cold chill shot up my back. I instinctively began to run toward her. My heart was pounding.

"Don't," I said. "Please don't."

I stopped when I drew close. She turned to face me.

"Why not?" she said.

I didn't want to say the wrong thing. I didn't want to make a mistake.

"Because, I know there's more here than you can see right now. I've been where you are. You need to discover who you are before you leave."

She looked at me as I moved toward her, reached out for my hand, and took a step back from the edge. I held her until she stopped shaking. We talked for hours at an all-night diner until I felt it was safe to drive her to her sister's place.

Years later, I saw her at a concert in the park. She was with a young girl about four or five who tugged on her sleeve.

"Mommy, do you know that man? He keeps smiling at you."

She glanced, then slowly recognized me. With tear filled eyes, she said, "I'd like you to meet my daughter, Hope."

Norma Jean Thornton

Her baby sister called her Nonie. Her great granddaughter calls her GumGum.

Norma Jean Thornton, also known as Nonie-Doodles, is an art-doodling, writing granny from Rio Linda, California, who, with unwanted help from her feisty cats, tries to dabble with her writing at the computer with one or more cats on the keyboard. She creates her doodle-art 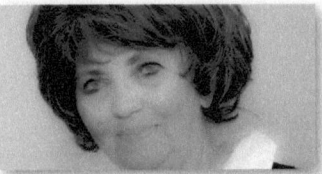 with a cat chewing on her pencil and fingers or lying on her paper. Her recipe books and volumes of doodle art have won accolades from sources no less than the California State Fair and professional book competitions.

Active in Northern California Publishers & Authors, she serves as communications director for the organization, and she is so well connected that she also serves as program chair, delivering top, publishing-industry talent and writers as speakers to monthly meetings.

NORMA JEAN THORNTON
Sweets for My Sweet

The chocolates. I know it was the chocolates. What other reason could there have been? He wouldn't let anyone else have any.

He had to have been slowly poisoning her with the candy.

"Sweets for my sweet," Father would always say as he gave her a new box of tasty morsels. They had me drooling.

Why wouldn't he bring some for me, too? I wondered.

When Mother opened the first box and offered me one, he grabbed the candy out of my hand.

"Those are just for your mother!" he quickly said.

Several weeks and several boxes of candy later, when I finally got a chance to sneak in and swipe one, I had a stomach ache and threw up for days—just like Mother had been doing for what seemed like forever.

It was so long ago. Questions lurked in my brain, never to be answered.

I had to push the worries farther and farther back because I couldn't tolerate the thoughts formulating in my mind, too unbearable to allow to surface. *What was going on?*

But then, what did I know? I was merely a child at the time. I so desperately worried about my mother I had little time to even think of such a possibility.

Besides, who could ever imagine her own father killing her mother—his wife, the supposed love of his life?

My two older siblings had already moved away from home.

My sister had married the year before, and my brother had gone into the Army about the same time.

That left me alone at home with Mother and Father.

I tried to ask my sister questions about our folks, but she didn't want to discuss it.

"If you ignore things, they'll just go away," she said.

My brother was no better. "Forget about it," he always said, "It's in the past and best forgotten."

That's not so. Those thoughts never go away, and you can never forget. Otherwise, why would I still be thinking about this now that I'm well over 80? It's too late to do anything about it since they're all gone now: Mother and Father, my brother and sister.

And my step-mother, whom Father married the day after mother died.

I'm old now. What do I know? Perhaps it wasn't the chocolates.

But then again, maybe it was?

"Sweets for my Sweets," he had always said.
Was it really sweets or poison, instead?
We always hope for the best, but we'll never know,
And wishful thinking doesn't make it so.

Nanci Ginsberg

Nanci Ginsberg grew up in the beautiful and historic Old Land Park area of Sacramento. Her family was extremely close-knit with many aunts, uncles, cousins, and grandparents living nearby. She was inspired by her grandmother, an artist, who painted with oils and gave Nanci art lessons.

Nanci naturally developed a life-long love of art. She started writing in poetry in 2002 and  successfully earned a host of publishing credits. In retirement, she obeyed her compulsion to write a children's book for her grandchildren, and she has now begun work on her first novel.

NANCI GINSBERG
Gloomy Days

It's dark outside, grey and hazy
trees stand so barren; like statues
cold and lonely, missing hues and vibrant colors
Just yesterday the trees were beautiful
showing their beauty of yellow and reds
glistening in the sunlight --
bringing smiles of contentment and awe.
The clouds are pillowy white
reminding everyone of angels with wings
Grey and dark gloom through the sky
making a dreary cold day with
thoughts of despair
feelings of emptiness and void
hopefully, the sun will appear again
renewing our inner strength of calm and serenity!

Springtime
Along The Delta

Springtime is here.

Barren trees transforming into
delicate buds of pink and white blossoms,

reflecting its colorful beauty upon
the still water-ways of the Delta. . .

Laurie Hoirup

Laurie Hoirup is the retired chief deputy director of the California State Council on Developmental Disabilities. Now fifty-nine, she has lived with a significant physical disability since the age of two, using a wheelchair since the age of five. She is diagnosed with spinal muscular atrophy (SMA2).

She lives in Sacramento with her husband.  She is the mother of two adult children and a grandmother. Her award-winning memoir *I Can Dance: My Life with a Disability*, is her first book, adding to her writing contributions found on Internet websites.

Learn more about her and see pictures of her growing up at www.LauriesLegacy.com.

LAURIE HOIRUP
Identical Irony

Taylor and Trinity were as close as any two sisters could be. As identical twins, born only one minute apart, they had a bond stronger than most siblings. Perhaps, someday, marriage and motherhood would change all that, but for now their attachment was solid.

To look at them, even standing side-by-side, you would swear to no difference in their appearances. Though they usually dressed their own way and wore varied hairstyles to be easily identified from one another, most people, other than their parents, could not tell them apart.

As youngsters, this provided the perfect framework for pulling jokes on friends and teachers. Thankfully, they were good girls and their pranks never mean or dishonest. On more than one occasion, they had traded places in class just to see what the other experienced. Though they were usually reprimanded, they never got into any real trouble because everything they did was in fun.

Every once in a while, they traded identities for a more serious reason. Once in fifth grade, Taylor stayed home sick on picture day, so Trinity had her photo taken twice with different hairstyles and clothing, ensuring Taylor would appear in the yearbook. They were always looking out for one another and doing their best to take care of each other. Their love for one another was apparent to all.

Throughout most of their years in school, they were often placed in different classrooms to prevent confusion. They agreed to this option because they preferred having their own identity and being recognized as themselves. By middle school, they had their own friends and their own preferences. Though they looked exactly alike, their personalities were opposite.

Taylor was outgoing, the social butterfly of the two. She loved sports and was a member of the cheer-leading squad for football. At the same time, she held her position as star goalie for the water polo team. She did well academically, carried a *B* average and could have probably done better if she were not so busy with her extra-curricular activities, which included the opposite sex.

Trinity, on the other hand, lived life shyly, more quiet and reserved. Walking in the park and communing with nature were her ideas of physical activity. She was a straight-*A* student and played the flute exceptionally well. She rarely dated, though she had plenty of male friends through Chess Club and through a volunteer, peer tutoring program—exactly the way she liked it.

Having interests and personalities as different as night and day would normally render two individuals totally incompatible. Yet Taylor and Trinity, despite their differences, were the best of friends, and their bond remained strong throughout the years. They were completely intrigued by one another's lives. Every night before bed, they would share their day's events and private thoughts with one another.

December arrived, and everyone was preparing for the up-coming, winter formal, except for Trinity who did not have a date—nor did she want one. This annual dance held no interest for her. Taylor, on the other hand, had already purchased her new gown and shoes, as well as selecting the young man she would accompany to the dance. However, things don't always turn out as planned.

To everybody's surprise, one of the most popular boys in school invited Trinity to the dance. Her first inclination was to say no, but her friends and parents urged her to accept. After all, she had to start dating sometime. Now was as good a time as any. Taylor promised to stay close at hand for anything she needed, which only added to the pressure of saying yes.

As the date drew near, Trinity, overwhelmed with cold feet, could not go through with it. She begged and pleaded with Taylor to come up with something to cancel her own date and fill in for her instead. This way, her classmates would believe she was dating, and her parents would not be disappointed in her. Besides, Taylor could get a date anytime she wanted. Missing the winter formal would not affect her popularity in the slightest. Surely Trinity would have the courage the next time around. She promised Taylor she would go through with it then. Of course, no one could know about this secret they shared, and they each knew the other would never tell.

Taylor eventually conceded, and the girls worked out a plan. On the day of the dance, Trinity, posing as Taylor, would feign illness and stay home in bed for the evening, appearing distraught about the turn of events. Taylor, posing as Trinity would go on to the dance with Trinity's date, appearing upset to be going without her popular sister for support.

The night worked out exactly as planned. "Taylor" stayed home sick in bed, nursing both a cold and bruised ego, while "Trinity" went out on her "first date," very anxious and hesitant. At least, that's what everyone thought, just as the girls wanted them to. They each played their parts so well none was the wiser.

Around midnight, a knock pounded on the door. The twin's father answered the door to find a police officer solemnly standing before him. He had brought tragic news: "Trinity" had been killed in a car accident.

Shocked, the parents sat wracked with grief and filled with guilt. If they hadn't pressured Trinity into going on this date, she would still be alive and home with them where she belonged. The true Trinity was consumed with her guilt; she had sent her sister in her place, and no one knew or even suspected. It was all her fault Taylor was gone. How would she ever tell her mother and father about this cruel and deceitful act? How would she ever live with herself?

Trinity held back the truth for days, trying to figure out the best way to let her parents know about this unfortunate switch. How do you let someone know that the daughter they loved so dearly and thought they lost was still with them.? How could she explain and the child they were holding onto so desperately now and believed to be with them was actually gone?

At the funeral, standing over a closed casket, her grieving mother sobbed hysterically and prayed.

"God, I would give anything to have Trinity back again, anything," she pleaded. Trinity held her mom close, deciding now was the best time to expose the truth; "Would you really, Mom?"

Jeff Parsons

J eff Parsons uses humor to help him avoid life's complications. Winning several humorous speech contests inspired Jeff to write, and for this book his humor comes through with recollections of grade-school relationships.

Alternatively, Jeff also writes horror stories to confront his fears. He has appeared in the *Bonded by Blood IV* and *V* anthologies. SNM Horror Magazine released Jeff's debut book of incredibly  scary stories, titled *Algorithm of Nightmares*, in December 2012.

When nothing works to make the monsters go away, Jeff bravely flees in terror, living to fight another day while eating lots of chocolate to console himself.

Despite all the evidence to the contrary, Jeff lives a reasonably quiet life within the fine city of Rocklin. Jeff_95630@yahoo.com is his email address.

JEFF PARSONS
Girls, I'm Clueless

I was invited to a party. Not just any party with cake, ice cream, and games. It was a party with girls attending. And, not just any girls. There'd be girls there who had preoccupied my attention for the longest time.

So why was this eight -ear-old geek anxious?

I had discovered that I was hopelessly fascinated, yet truly clueless when it came to the opposite sex. And, truth be told, that condition hasn't improved significantly over time.

Something magical had happened to me when I was four.

I was a young kid with nothing much to obsessively preoccupy my mind except for the logical fear of nighttime; that was when the world grew dark and the monsters came out. That scared me. Until I learned about girls; they scared me even more.

I'd just moved from the big city to the suburbs. Actually, my parents did the moving and I came along for the ride like needy carry-on baggage that whined a lot.

My new life landed me in the suburbs where everything sprawled raw and exposed, where large swathes of ground lay uncovered by buildings, concrete, garbage, and graffiti. Suburban wilderness—what could happen in an uncivilized place like this?

Well, I'll tell you…

Yes, girls were involved. Not just one or two. Three, I tell you. Diane and Leslie, who were identical twins, and Suzanne.

Like all unexpected things, it just happened.

We were playing in the grassy side yard of my house.

The three cuties in my story, four-year-old girls whom I'd met a few short months ago, were already far more mature than I was. They suggested playing a game called Fairies.

Why are they giggling? I wondered.

The Fairies game involved fairy princesses. They were held captive, by whom or what I didn't know, but I should have asked before getting involved. Maybe their free spirits were imprisoned by common sense.

A powerful, magical spell compelled them to perform endless ballroom dances, swirling gracefully about, bedecked in imaginary, flowing, princess gowns.

"Help us! Set us free!" Diane pleaded. The others echoed her chant.

I was the fairy prince, apparently honor-bound to set them free.

"What do I do?" I asked, intrigued, but struggling out of my depth.

"You have to kiss us," Suzanne, the closest fairy, replied.

"Uh, okay," I shrugged and did it. I kissed Suzanne without a thought, totally swept up in the moment by my method-acting role.

The other two girls gasped in pretend shock and awe. Suzanne kissed me back in return —not just once, but three more times, grabbing my cheeks with both hands and pulling me in for some big wet ones. Finally, she left me with a smile, joining the other girls in a giggling fest.

Flabbergasted, I watched them swirl gracefully away, out of my yard, into the street, and out of sight, taking their bubbly laughter with them.

Uh, what just happened? I kissed her! Ohhhh, then *ewwwwww!* Or so I thought, defaulting to preschool thoughts that revolved around "uh, I don't know" and other mind-numbing variants thereof. Actually, a small, quiet part of me was excited, and I thought about future possibilities.

It wasn't until much later that I realized that they had manipulated me – I knew that without even knowing what the word 'manipulated' meant. Not that I was complaining, but *how could they do that?* They were clever indeed; even though, to be honest, it clearly didn't take much to fool me. I couldn't even figure out how to talk, let alone outsmart anyone.

Here's the truly weird part. After that erotic episode, they'd only have to glance at me and then start chuckling. Apart from that, they didn't interact with me much at all, except for occasionally staring at me with googly eyes (technical term: eyes longing for something, probably something involving more derisive laughter directed at me).

Whenever I attempted feeble conversation, a skill I'd mastered long ago, nothing came out of it.

They'd roll their eyes and tell me I was sooooo silly.

Okay, I was lost. What did they want me to do? I had no idea – maybe they wanted me to chase after them, catch them and kiss them, perhaps in that order? The idea terrified me and there was no hiding it. And still, they played that shy, elusive staring game with me every time thereafter.

Actually, to this day, I still don't know what I was supposed to do.

So, fast forward to eight years old.

The party would start after school at Suzanne's house. I was excited that I was allowed to stay outside beyond my curfew time even if I had to keep a wary eye out for monsters. So much freedom – whatever would I do with it?

I was clueless to say the least.

What to wear? How to act? What to say? All these thoughts were beyond me. I was still working on 'how to breath' when I was around these girls. Somehow, they had become very interesting to me. Perhaps it was because they could talk intelligently or were eons more mature than I was or maybe I was fascinated by the lingering memory of an old fairy tale game.

With some underlying trepidation, I went to the party. No presents required. Just bring myself and have fun eating cake and ice cream. No problem.

Still...

Early darkness lurked in the shadows when I arrived at Suzanne's house. The rockin' sound of funky music did little to reassure me as I ambled down a pathway and entered the flood-lit backyard party.

Before me, on a red picnic table, there was a huge sheet cake, a cooler, utensils, and plates. Inside the cooler, there were three tubs of ice cream: vanilla, vanilla and vanilla flavored. Kids filled up their plates with gobs of ice cream and slabs of cake. I'd never seen sheet cake before – it reminded me of the Styrofoam material that made up the plates and cooler, but it had less texture and actually tasted better.

Not a parent in sight…they must be having some cocktails inside the house.

The attendees were odd kids from around the block. They provided a wide variety of first impressions: runny noses, milk mustaches, quirky ticks, impulsively idiotic, attention-getting irritating, and quiet as a fart in church.

I fit right in. Below my tightly belted waistline, I wore stiff shorts that flared out like the tail end of a Saturn V booster rocket. Dirty socks in Ked's sneakers – for me, no more Frankenstein black leather shoes (once upon a time, they were a cure for my flat feet). Dress shirt, mussed up, half in, half out of my shorts, there was probably another half around somewhere that I've never found.

My friend Phillip waved to me. He was the worldly type who knew about girls. In contrast, he also had ice cream smeared around his lips and chin. That was typical of him. Completely at ease – his mind mercifully free of self-awareness.

The three girls, Suzanne, Diane, and Leslie, had been eye-balling me at least a good half-minute before I noticed them. They smiled cryptically.

Oh my god. My heart stuttered. [Thump… thump, thump, thump…]

I strolled to the table in my best imitation of cool (which is to say, I dragged my feet and stumbled on an unseen patio step). I then went through sloppy motions of putting too much cake and ice cream onto a flimsy plate.

I then retreated to where Phillip stood on the periphery of the party.

"Nice party. I like food," he said, being deep and mysterious.

"Uh-yeah, I eat food, too," I replied, distracted, feeling like I was being emotionally dissected by the staring girls. "When do we do it?"

"When I say so."

"Uh, okay."

We talked about the usual inane things while the chaos of other young children blazed out of control around us. Unlimited access to raw sugar, lack of direct parental supervision, unbridled random activities and the thrill of nighttime approaching made this event quite the zoo at feeding time.

After calmly observing the spectacle of bedlam erupting around them, the three girls left the backyard, glancing over their shoulders to snicker at me. They sashayed away down the pathway, which was something I wasn't sure how to take, let alone understand.

They were probably going to talk about intellectual things, like the incredibly immature behavior of boys.

"Now," Phillip belched with perfect diction.

"Huh?"

"Now," he said, without gas.

"What?"

"Go hide now. In the bushes," he said, exasperated, index finger wagging to the appropriate bushes near the pathway to make it clearer.

"Oh, the plan. Right."

I put my plate on the food table as casually as I could (fail), but, no one noticed my social faux pas – most of the kids were scurrying amok in a sugar-frenzied high.

As I entered the bushes, I noticed that the pathway to the front of the house had grown dark with shadows. Unfortunately, it was even darker inside the bushes...*yikes*.

I went through a mental checklist to distract myself from thinking about the monsters who were definitely creeping up on me in the darkness.

Phillip said the plan had to run like magic - timing was everything.

Easy as one, two, three...

One. I was to pretend to be the Wolfman. We'd seen the movie at a school film fest. It was wicked scary.

Two. I'd jump out of the bushes and spook the three girls.

Three. They'd react appropriately. Shrieks and squeals. Phillip and I would laugh.

The end result: the girls would think we're sooooo clever and suddenly like us.

I didn't think it through much further than that – alas, our plan reflected the zenith of moronic reasoning. Actually, it was Phillips plan, but he was okay with sharing the glory with me as long as I did all the hard work.

In my mind, I kept replaying his words from yesterday at the playground: "You want to get their attention?" That's an embarrassing question for me to answer, mind you, torn between wanting their attention and having to admit brazenly that I liked these girls. He had whispered those words to me, along with other ones about a plan, while the girls talked among each other, not far away. Phillip was a little deaf and I was a little stupid, so the conversation wasn't at all subtle. I checked to see if we were overheard by the girls. Nope, they kept on talking amongst themselves... something about boys being stinky, I think.

I tortured myself while I waited in the bushes. *Do I really want to do this?*

Then, the moment of decision.

The three girls were returning to the backyard. Completely unaware of me, they were quite lively, as if sharing yet another joke amongst themselves.

I'd certainly take them by surprise.

But, what if I behaved like a fool? Oh wait, I'm usually foolish anyway...

Do it!

I leaped out of the bushes, onto the pathway, arms stretched out, hands drawn into gnarly claw shapes, back hunched over, eyes wild and teeth bared.

"Rooowww-urrrr," I growled, with a drool of slobber, in retrospect realizing I should've practiced the part beforehand. In my ears, it sounded pathetic, like an involuntary sound I once made just before throwing up.

The girls thought differently of my performance. Eyes wide. Staggering several steps backward. Hands drawn up to mouths. Screams peeling. Sobbing and crying ensued.

Oh my God. What have I done?

Then, something ab-so-lute-ly horrible happened.

Suzanne clutched her chest and slouched onto the concrete pathway. She was breathing like a fish out of water, wide gulping breaths like she couldn't get enough air. She passed out, not breathing, body sagging like a deflated balloon.

Phillip had appeared at my side. "What have you done?" he whispered in a terrified, yet quietly amazed tone.

A sudden chilly sweat made me feel numb and disconnected.

Suzanne was out cold on the pathway. The twins, Diane, and Leslie, resorting to helpless panic, wailed, "You killed her," simultaneously, with that strange twin's mannerism.

My heartbeat fluttered. *No.*

By now, I sensed the other kids approaching the scene of the tragic accident.

"Murderer. She had a heart addition," Diane blurted out. A 'heart addition' was really a 'heart condition', but I knew what she meant anyway. I watched enough television to know that at least.

"Save her. You have to save her!" Leslie squealed, latching onto my trembling arm and pulling me close to Suzanne.

"Wu-what?" I responded, dumbfounded. After all, being a murderer was something new to me. One trapped-and-going-crazy part of my mind imagined doing hard time in the lockup: no ice cream, comic books or cartoons.

"She needs recess… mouth to mouth," Diane pleaded with me.

Ah, that thing on television.

I killed Suzanne. It was up to me to bring her back to life.

Kneeling down next to her head, I grabbed her head and went in.

I touched her lips with mine (the ancient memory returning unbidden). I breathed into her.

Nothing.

Again.

Nothing.

Again.

Nothing.

Again – some movement, she wrapped her arms around me while I was breathing into her.

She held me tight. And kissed me!

She held me lip locked for an eternity. I was surprised, to say the least, and off balance in more than one way. It was… incredible.

What? She's not dead? Yay!

Then, I heard the laughter of the other children around us, especially Diane and Leslie, the evil twins, who were howling with laughter in my peripheral vision, painfully so, bent over, legs crossed and holding an arm out to each other for support.

Phillip looked confused.

I was also confused until Suzanne winked at me. "I knew you wanted that..." she said, dead-pan serious for a second before springing up to join the twins, and the three of them just about peed their pants as they exploded into further hysterical gales of laughter.

I was setup? No way...

I looked at Philip. He grinned like an idiot at the other kids around us, "Uh, yeah, we knew all about that. We was just going along with it."

The girls must've overheard us. On the playground. Wow...

Life after that was less confusing for me, still awkward mind you, but less confusing when it came to my dealings with the fairer sex. I realized then that I was, and probably always will be, in no way capable of keeping up with the wily intelligence of girls...

Tom Kando

Tom Kando, PhD, grew up in World War II Europe, spending his formative years in Paris and Amsterdam. At eighteen, he came to America as a lonely immigrant and a Fulbright student. He became a professor at major universities, taught in prisons, and lectured worldwide. His memoir, *A Tale of Survival*, describes his far-flung and sometimes harrowing experiences.

He has authored articles about crime, terrorism, psychology, sports, and travel in the *Wall Street Journal,* the *Los Angeles Examiner* and other venues, plus nine books, including *Leisure and Popular Culture, Social Interaction* (C.V. Mosby), *Sexual Behavior and Family Life* (Elsevier), and *Readings in Criminology* (Kendall Hunt).

He lives in Gold River, California. His website is www.TomKando.com.

TOM KANDO

It's an Omelet Thing

International travel is marvelous. Exciting experiences and beautiful sights contrast with the drudgery of everyday life. But sometimes a traveler encounters things that are frustrating, incomprehensible, unreasonable, and unworkable.

Recently my wife Anita and I spent more than a month in Europe. I first flew to Amsterdam. My 102-year-old mother lives in Holland, so I visit as often as I can to help her.

Then, Anita joins me, and we tack on some tourism to my filial responsibilities. We usually go south for a few weeks, to France, Italy and surrounding venues. Paris often ends up on our itinerary because I grew up there. I still know people there, so a return to the City of Lights is always difficult to resist.

As usual, we took the marvelous Talys bullet train to Paris (also known as the "TGV," for *Train a Tres Grande Vitesse*). The smooth, luxury ride from Holland to Paris's *Gare du Nord* takes only four hours. Feeling as if you were floating on cushions, you race by cars driving down the autoroute, easily going twice their speed, realizing that you are traveling at the speed of an airplane, not of ground transportation. Talys attendants come by and serve free, gourmet meals and wines. The seats and leg space are so comfortable that sleep is inevitable at some point. If only airlines could emulate some of this! This is the form of transportation a majority of Californians and other Americans consider a waste of money. Japan just celebrated its bullet train's fiftieth anniversary. China has built several thousand miles of high-speed train tracks.

Dozens of countries have or are in the process of developing, high-speed trains, including Poland, Spain, and Korea which Americans smugly feel superior to. I often fear that ignorance and insularity will be America's downfall.

But I'm getting carried away. A key point of this travelogue is precisely the opposite, namely that travel in Europe is *not* all sunshine and roses. Many things are far from hunky-dory. Some things work way better than in America, but some don't.

* * *

We arrive in Paris early afternoon. The gorgeous City of Lights is often where the difficulties start.

For one thing, the French continue to often treat people badly (although this may be a characteristic of Parisians, more than all Frenchmen). I am sorry to have to say this. I am practically French myself. My French accent is still flawless. When I visit, people ask me which French city I am from. I am a Francophile. I taught French at the university. I believe that French music, painting, and literature are second to none.

But, the French are difficult people—no doubt about it. France is like a gorgeous and high-maintenance woman. It is what it is.

Paris hotels are incredibly expensive, even the thousands of hotels whose rooms are small, mediocre, ugly, and uncomfortable. We had reserved a room at a hotel recommended by famed travel adviser Rick Steves, figuring that one can hardly go wrong doing so. It was in the Seventh Arrondissement, near the Eiffel Tower. The neighborhood and the street were darling, but when we entered our room, it turned out to be a dark, bathroom-sized cubicle on the backside of the hotel, having one small bed and a window looking out on a dirty stone wall close enough to touch it. This for one-hundred-forty-nine euros per night. The hotel's name was Le Grand Leveque, but there was nothing grand about it.

I immediately told the registration clerk that this room was unacceptable. I asked for a better room, whatever the cost might be. All she had was a front-side room with a fine view over the beautiful Rue Cler but with three beds, and, thus, expensive. We had no choice but to suck it up and pay the one-hundred-euro surcharge for a total fee of two-hundred-fifty euros per night.

The alternative would have been to leave and lug our suitcases around Paris, looking for a better deal.

Anita and I have a new expression: "It's an omelet thing." This means that you can't make an omelet without breaking eggs. So whenever we meet with some adversity, we chalk it up as a minor, inevitable but not catastrophic setback. For example, last year in Rome a couple of punks tried to rob me of my briefcase. I gave chase and retrieved my briefcase, but not without messing up my clothes and getting scratched up. I was satisfied with the outcome.

So now we were in Paris, paying more for a mediocre hotel room than I had ever paid for a hotel room in my life. But this was just another omelet thing. We decided to enjoy ourselves and be happy. We had four wonderful days. We heard a marvelous string quintet play Vivaldi's Four Seasons and other hits at the Madeleine, we visited the Orangerie, which still houses the best Monet frescoes, we ate like royalty every night, we shopped at the amazing Galeries Lafayette, we strolled in the Luxembourg Gardens, and more.

Then came the day when we had to take the TGV again, this time down to Toulouse, France's fourth-largest city, located in the country's Southwest. We wanted to use Toulouse as a base and drive around the surrounding region, called the Languedoc, for about a week. We planned to visit such places as Albi, a beautiful medieval town which also features the famous Toulouse Lautrec museum, the ancient walled city of Carcassonne, and other places.

As I said, travel is marvelous. However, the transitions can often be exhausting and traumatic, especially as one gets older. Anita and I have some standing jokes about this. We often wish that we could be beamed to our destinations, as in "Beam me up, Scotty." Also, do you remember the old Greyhound Bus slogan "Getting there is half the fun?" What a crock! Anita says that getting there is often *none* of the fun. I agree.

Next, we had to go to Paris' Gare Montparnasse to take the Toulouse TGV. Montparnasse is one of those gigantic Paris railroad stations with dozens of platforms crowded with thousands of passengers running in dozens of directions.

And one thing that makes European travel often nerve-racking is this: At railroad stations as well as at airports, the departure platform is not announced until mere minutes before departure. Hundreds of people all stand underneath an enormous board on which departure platform or gate numbers suddenly appear, often less than ten minutes before departure time. When the information finally begins to flash, hundreds of people stampede toward the relevant gate.

The situation is worse at railroad stations than at airports because seats are reserved for a specific car. After you've finally figured out where each car's number is posted, you discover that yours is at the front of the train, a third of a mile away. So you run as fast as you can, pulling your suitcases, crashing into other passengers, and rolling over their feet. They do the same things to you. This time, it could have come to blows. I accidentally bumped into a Frenchman who was running with a baby in his arms. He tried to kick me, but only managed to kick my suitcase. Afraid that we would miss the train, I kept my hands to myself and didn't pursue the issue.

I had planned our trip meticulously: The TGV was leaving Paris at noon. It was to arrive in Toulouse around 6 p.m. There we would pick up an Avis rental, drive to Albi about an hour away, and check in at our hotel no later than 8 p.m., still well before dark.

Alas, we encountered another omelet situation: after a smooth five-hour ride across the scenic French countryside and miles of vineyards, the train came to a halt in the middle of nowhere. For the next several hours, it didn't budge. The cause? Cattle had crossed the tracks, and some were killed. There was a mess to clean up.

I began to fret about our timetable. How late was the Avis office in Toulouse open? What would our hotel in Albi do if it got to be real late and we still hadn't shown up? A friendly train employee called the hotel for us. We learned we could arrive at any time of the night.

Finally the train resumed its course. We reached the Avis car rental in Toulouse after dark, but they were still open. We got a fine, little, four-door Audi with standard shift. Our next challenge was to find our way to the town of Albi and our hotel.

Driving a car, visitors have three ways to find their way around: paper maps, road signs, and GPS.

Maps are difficult to come by these days. Car rental companies don't even give them out. Even though I absolutely love maps, I rarely carry them in my car anymore.

Road signs are essential. Without them, you are lost.

But realistically today, it's all about GPS (quaintly branded a Tom Tom in Europe, after the Dutch company that manufactures most European GPS units). Sometimes your rented car has GPS; sometimes the agencies extort an extra thirty euros a day for it. Either way, I haven't bothered figuring out how the rented car's GPS works, nor do I use my iPhone's GPS. Instead, I rely on a Garmin which we bought for one-hundred-twenty dollars at Costco about five years ago. We always bring it to Europe with us, along with the required eurochip.

After our Garmin acquires the satellites, it knows what it's doing—sometimes. The fact that the lady mispronounces foreign names is only amusing. But quite often the Garmin and the local road signs are at odds with each other. Usually, the Garmin tries to guide us to our destination by the shortest route, but frequently, she doesn't know that this requires taking an impassable dirt mountain road or trespassing through some construction site. Sometimes she tells us to turn right onto a road twenty feet below us which we are crossing on a freeway overpass. Other times she tells us to turn left just as a sign tells us to go straight ahead. So whenever our Garmin and a road sign disagree, we go with the sign.

We exit the Avis garage a little after 8 p.m. It's pitch dark, and we are somewhere on the outskirts of Toulouse International Airport in Blagnac. It is enormous and confusing, because this is where Airbus is located—the largest aircraft manufacturer in the world. We are utterly and totally lost. We are surrounded by gigantic hangars, construction sites, barriers, and fences separating us from runways, one-way streets, and dead-end streets. The Garmin cannot save us. It can only endlessly recalculate.

We come by a lone, empty-but-still-open eating joint. I barge in, panicked, and scream at the cook, a boyish young man, "Where are we? How do I get to the road to Albi?" The boy gives me some advice. After meandering in the dark for another ten minutes, a miracle occurs: A road sign emerges, posting: "To Albi!"

We get to our hotel in Albi an hour before midnight. A nice, receptionist is waiting for us. We are ravenous, and she suggests a Turkish eatery around the corner. "Worth a try, even at this hour," I say. When we arrive, the owner is just shutting down, but he reopens the kitchen just for us. We eat some fine kebabs and salad with feta cheese. Besides us, the eatery hosts a drunken Frenchman finishing his *ouzo*. He insists on a conversation with us, or actually more a monologue: He slurs together something about the great *Albigensian Heresy* and the Catholic crusade against it in which many were killed.

The following week, we learned more about this fascinating period of medieval history. Anita and I headed to Carcassonne and other cities along the foot of the snow- capped Pyrenees. The people of this region became adherents of *Catharism*, an alternative to Catholicism. The pope declared this a heresy. A bloody crusade ensued, culminating in the massacre of dozens of thousands of Cathars in 1209.

A week later, we fly from Toulouse to Rome for our final week in Europe. That becomes another exquisite week filled with Fabio's cooking classes, outdoor concerts in the Teatro Marcello, picnics in Aqueduct Park, Trajan's Marketplace and the Campo de Fiori fountain, visits to sights we have not previously seen, such as Cinecitta, Eataly, the newly opened houses of Augustus and Livia Drusilla, along with obligatory return visits to the Capitoline Museum, and the Forum. But I'll stop right here, just to say that if Paris is Catherine Deneuve or Brigitte Bardot, Rome is Sophia Loren or Gina Lollobrigida. How can you choose?

***

What makes European travel complicated is that there are so many countries, each obedient to unique time schedules, regulations, and customs. For example, when are various shops open, and where do you buy various items?

In France, Italy and some other countries, shoppers buy postage stamps and bus tickets at the tobacco shop. How on earth would American visitors know this? Anita and I joke that perhaps we could buy toilet paper at the shoemaker, books at the bakery, or newspapers at the butcher shop?

And speaking of butchers, France has three kinds: the *charcuterie*, where you buy processed meats such as salami and paté; the *boucherie*, where you buy your raw meat, such as cuts of beef or veal or hamburger; and the *boucherie chevaline*, where you buy horse meat. The latter is always recognizable by a statue of a horse head in front of the store.

But things get even more complicated; in France, most

groceries and other food stores are closed on Monday. On the other hand, huge department stores like the Galeries Lafayette are closed on Sunday.

In Rome, it's the museums that are closed on Monday. Except that some sites are closed on Tuesday, such as Cinecitta and the Baths of Caracalla. Then, some attractions are closed period, because they are being repaired. This was my experience with the Trevi fountain. I have gone to sites only to find that they were closed so many times that I now have a new rule of thumb: "Any museum, site or store will be closed on the day Tom Kando wants to visit it."

Another issue is *space*. Eating lunch at a Paris sidewalk restaurant is risky. Your sidewalk table is about two-by-two feet in size. Hotel rooms are equally minuscule. I read somewhere that Paris has the highest population density of any major city. I suppose Europe's population density is still considerably higher than ours. Also, culturally, Europeans' personal space is smaller than ours. They don't mind smelling each other as much as Americans do.

Also contributing to hotel discomfort are the inadequate showers, which often malfunction and sometimes flood the entire bathroom floor. Some hotels, at least in the provinces, advertise swimming pools and Jacuzzis. Typically, the Jacuzzis will be ice cold.

The bathroom problem is perennial: Free, public bathrooms are not something Europeans believe in. I have often wondered why Europeans don't seem to have a need to pee. The twelve million people of greater Paris probably share seventeen public bathrooms together. The same in Rome. If you are so lucky as to find one, it'll cost you at least one and a half euro. That's two dollars to take a pee! In recent years, the number of public bathrooms has increased a bit. Jot this down: there is one right behind the Colosseum, and one by the Southwest foot of the Eiffel Tower.

Have you ever tried to use a café's bathroom without ordering a drink? Sometimes, you *have* to go, and you run into a café, no matter what. Then, all hell breaks loose. They are likely to become physically abusive. I did this once in Switzerland; a waitress blocked the bathroom door to prevent access. In Germany, after I came out of a bathroom, a waiter grabbed me by the shoulder. In France, after Anita made an emergency stop in a restaurant, several waiters began insulting her and jeering as she walked out.

And then there are the airline problems. On this trip, the problems included a strike by Air France pilots. Europeans like to strike. There was also a strike by Roman bus and metro employees. Only our Toulouse-Rome flight happened to be on Air France. Luckily, our flight was not one of the fifty-eight percent of all flights canceled.

On our return to the United States, innumerable things went wrong: While we had Delta tickets, the flight was operated by Alitalia. This confused everyone, including the taxi driver who took us out to Fumicino Airport. He assured us that *all* U.S.-bound international fights and *all* Delta flights depart from Terminal One, and that's where he dropped us off. But he was wrong. We had to rush to the Alitalia terminal number Five. Because time was running out, we paid a cab another twenty dollars to drive us half a mile to the correct terminal.

Next surprise: The airline did not honor our two, reserved adjacent seats. Anita and I were separated for the entire thirteen-hour flight between Rome and Los Angeles flight. Anita found herself sitting a half-dozen rows in front of me.

Oh well, at least the meals were good. In the food department, Alitalia sure beats all the American airlines. But I didn't quite understand what they meant when their menu proudly announced that they served purely "biological bread." Hmm...

The connection to our Los Angeles-Sacramento flight was a near-disaster. As a veteran, overseas traveler, I know the routines that transpire when I return home.

Because there are no direct flights from Sacramento to Europe, I always have to connect somewhere, for example Minneapolis, Atlanta, or Los Angeles. When Americans return home from foreign travel, they must always go through customs at the port of re-entry into the US (for example, Minneapolis, Atlanta and Los Angeles are ports of re-entry).

Before taking the connecting local flight to Sacramento, we would have to pass through customs, even if our baggage were checked all the way to Sacramento. So in making plans, we decided to fly by way of Los Angeles and leave at least two hours before boarding our connecting flight.

However, Homeland Security had just introduced a newfangled

system whereby every international passenger upon arrival has to undergo an eye scan, be photographed, and then turn the photo over to a customs officer. All of this can take very long, as the crowds are often enormous. Think of an Airbus 380 from Europe disgorging more than eight-hundred-fifty passengers all at once!

Unfortunately on this occasion, Delta moved our connecting flight's departure up by half an hour, leaving us with barely an hour and a half to go through the customs, passport, and the eye-scan procedures. We had to run like mad from one terminal to another at crappy LA International, our hearts palpitating and swimming in our sweat.

But the most disturbing experience upon arrival in Los Angeles was our brief "Auschwitz moment." We and hundreds of other international passengers were to be ushered to an escalator up to a landing, then through double glass doors, and down a hallway. However, the double glass doors on top of the escalator were locked! Meanwhile, dozens of deplaning passengers kept coming up the escalator every minute and joining the increasingly crowded, small landing area from which there was no escape. I was already looking around to see where Anita and I could best position ourselves, somewhere at the periphery maybe. Luckily, an employee arrived and unlocked the double door before a catastrophic stampede could occur.

Flying has become increasingly nightmarish over the decades. While I have occasionally been upgraded to first class or business, I am not rich enough to fly that way most of the time. And for the masses of us who fly economy, travel is becoming a form of torture.

***

But I don't want to end negatively. While Greyhound is wrong in asserting that "getting there is half the fun," *being there* is still a blast.

It starts with the gorgeous cities, architecture and culture. That's what tourism is all about, of course. Jewel cities like Albi abound in Europe.

Every time we go overseas, we meet wonderful, friendly, and helpful people. This time, in Toulouse, a handsome young Senegalese boy not only gave us directions in the subway, but also walked with us and took us to our destination.

Another amazing thing overseas is the public transportation infrastructure. In addition to the marvelous long-distance train system, even mid-size cities like Toulouse support state-of the-art subways.

In addition, their medical services are good, efficient, and dirt cheap. Two years ago in Paris, I developed a minor infection. The hotel steered me to a doctor two blocks away. Within an hour, the doctor had seen me, and I had the antibiotic he prescribed. Total cost for everything? Forty dollars.

The food is often great, sometimes divine. Every region of France has its own cuisine. This year, we sampled the Languedoc's specialty, which is a cassoulet, a stew with sausage, duck and beans. The cassoulet at Albi's La Fourchette Adroite was to die for. Last year we were in Gascony, which is paté country. Italy has more kinds of pasta and pizza than can be listed even in Wikipedia.

The regional dialects and accents are a never-ending source of wonder to me. In Toulouse, everyone sounds exactly like Cesar (Yves Montand) and Ugolin (Daniel Auteuil) in the unforgettable movie *Jean De Florette*. How can one not want to go back to such places over and over again?

Ellen Osborn

Ellen Osborn is the author of *A Lovely & Comfortable Heritage Lost*, a unique history of El Dorado County beginning with the early days of the gold rush and the first conflicts with the Native American tribes of the region.

Her book also traces the evolution of California's Highway 50 from its beginning as the Native American trade trail that became a popular Gold Rush route. Her book explains why it has come to be called one of the most storied and romantic roads in American history.

Most importantly, Osborn shares the story of her great grandfather, John Calhoun Johnson, and the world he lived in as emigrants poured into California seeking promises of riches and following their own dreams of a new life.

She says she wrote the following story, "Hercules the Mighty Hunter," so that her grandson Robert could know the gentle, loving people who were his great grandparents and something about the world as it was.

ELLEN OSBORN

Hercules
the Mighty Hunter

My parents' first real home after they were married was a little house in Sacramento. They lived there all by themselves because we children hadn't been born yet. To liven up their home, they wanted to adopt a kitten. It wasn't hard to find someone with a mommy cat who had kittens ready to go to new homes. My parents visited the people who had the mommy cat and kittens. There were lots of kittens chasing and climbing and wrestling each other. It was hard to choose. There were striped kittens and spotted kittens. But Mother and Dad spied a little gray kitten, smaller than the rest. He was shy and seemed to trip over his own feet. That was the one they wanted.

They gently carried him home to their little house. On the way, they discussed what to name him. They decided on Hercules after the Hercules of legend, the famous strongman. They laughed at their little joke because their new kitten was far from being big and strong. He was just a purring little ball of fur.

Mother bustled about arranging food and water bowls and making a warm, welcoming bed for their new kitten. Meanwhile, Hercules explored his new world, climbing under and over all the furniture. Mother made cat toys, too. From her knitting basket, she rolled brightly colored yarn into small balls, each with a prize inside: a crumpled scrap of paper for Hercules to bat around.

The next day Dad had to go to work. He said good-bye to Mother and Hercules and drove away in their big gray Dodge car. He drove downtown to the state capital building where he worked as an auditor for the Division of Highways. Mother was a stay-at-home housewife as many women were in the days before World War II. That day was special for her because instead of being alone all day, she now had the companionship of Hercules. Mother took careful note of all of Hercules's antics so she could share them with Dad when he came home in the evening.

Hercules thrived in his new home. He grew quickly and played constantly, weaving crazy webs of blue and red yarn around the legs of the chairs. He pounced on the crumpled bits of paper as though they were mice, chasing them around until he tired of them, and then pushed the little bits of paper under the bookcase. He must have heard about flying carpets because when he would make a great leap onto the throw rug, both kitten and rug would skid across the polished-wood floor, flying all the way to the wall. When he exhausted himself playing, Hercules would curl up on his favorite sofa cushion, the one where the morning sunlight warmed him, and he would fall asleep.

It was about this time that Mother and Dad discovered they hadn't adopted a boy kitty. They had a girl kitty! Hercules was not a he. Hercules was a she! What to do? Hercules was not a name for a girl, but Hercules already knew her name. It would be confusing to change it. They settled on Herky, and so it was from that day on.

As a grown cat, Herky showed great skill as a hunter. She proudly displayed mice she had killed on the back steps. Sometimes she caught birds. Herky cleaned all the fish out of the pond in the garden and then went to work on the neighbor's fish pond. She was a sight to see as she heaved herself and fish over the back fence, bringing her kill home to enjoy. Mother and Dad couldn't deny it was their cat doing the mischief when they found a fish skeleton on their lawn! Nevertheless, Mother was so proud of her sleek, strong cat: Herky the Mighty Hunter.

Mother did most of her grocery shopping at the neighborhood grocery store, a place she could walk to because she didn't drive. There were no supermarkets then. That was the way most housewives shopped in those days. The neighborhood grocery stores, usually located on a corner, were small, but had a little bit of everything. Mother shopped often because she had to limit her purchases to what she could carry the two and a half blocks home.

The owner of the grocery store was a stocky man who always

wore a wide, white apron wrapped around his big stomach and tied in the back. It started out white but quickly became stained and streaked with red as he cut up meat for his customers. He would grind hamburger right there in his store. The customer would select a piece of meat, and the grocer would put it through his big shiny meat grinder. The grocer knew all his customers and liked to chat with everyone.

One Friday morning, Mother stopped in for some groceries for the weekend. The grocery store was only open on weekdays and not at night. You had to plan ahead so you wouldn't run out of anything you needed on Saturday or Sunday. That is why ladies were always borrowing things such as cups of sugar from their neighbors.

This particular morning, the grocer was in a bad mood. Hungry mice were overrunning his little store. The mice would sneak in at night and on the weekends when the grocer was absent. They would bite holes in bags of rice or beans, spilling the contents on the floor. Crackers were a favorite with the mice, so crackers were spilled on the floor too. Mingled in the mess of wasted food were little black pellets of mice droppings. The grocer quickly swept up the evidence of the previous night's invasion. It wouldn't do for his customers to see this unsanitary mess. He complained to Mother that the mice were getting bolder and ignoring the traps he had set.

Mother was sympathetic and wanted to help. She said, "What you need is a cat, a cat that is a good mouser like my Herky." So proud of her Herky that, with a rush of enthusiasm, she offered to let the grocer borrow Herky. They struck an agreement that Mother would bring Herky at closing time that day. Herky would be locked in the store for the weekend to catch as many mice as she could. Mother was confident it would be many.

If Mother had any misgivings about this arrangement or any second thoughts, she still delivered Herky as promised. After getting Herky settled for the weekend, she went home alone to a very quiet house. She still had to explain to Dad where their cat was and convince him Herky was doing a great service for the grocery store and the neighborhood in general. Dad was a very quiet man who kept his thoughts to himself, so we don't know how he felt about this arrangement.

By Sunday, Mother felt anxious. She walked to the grocery

store to peek through the window to see how Herky was doing. She gasped in horror. She saw an even bigger mess than the mice had made. Evidence everywhere indicated a great chase had taken place. In addition to rice, beans, and crackers strewn about, a large pool of pickle brine flooded the floor, fallen from a huge crock that always sat on the counter.

Looking past the dripping, pickle brine and ignoring the tipped-over displays of cans and boxes, Mother finally saw Herky. There she was, standing on the big, wooden chopping block where the grocer cut meat for his customers. She enjoyed licking the rich, meaty flavors that clung to the wooden surface. Embarrassed, Mother went home, but she resolved to be there Monday morning when the grocer arrived so she could claim Herky and help repair the damage.

She arrived too late. The grocer had arrived even earlier and was already inside the store surveying the wreckage. In a meek voice, Mother asked where Herky was. From his expression, it was clear that the grocer didn't know and didn't care. He said when he unlocked and opened the door, the cat streaked by him and disappeared.

The grocer accepted Mother's apologies and waved her away to look for her cat as he went to work to restore order before more store customers arrived. Mother secretly hoped he wouldn't notice that the butcher block had been carefully cleaned by Herky's little, pink, tongue. At that moment, it was the cleanest place in the store.

Mother spent most of the day, as she would the next several days, fruitlessly searching for Herky. Dad helped her in the evenings. Finally, she gave up. There were no more places to look. Mother felt so bad. All she was trying to do was help, but everything went wrong. The grocer was still annoyed with her. Dad was sad because he loved all animals, but especially Herky, and Mother missed her cat.

Almost two weeks later, Mother thought she heard a "meow." She rushed to open the door, not daring to hope, and there was Herky! She stood thinner and rather dirty, but she definitely was Herky. Mother bent down, gently picked up her cat and carried her into the house. Setting Herky down, Mother hurried to fill her long-empty, food bowl, adding a treat consisting of a bowl of cream. Herky ate it all. When she could hold no more, Herky sought her favorite sofa cushion, the one warmed by the morning sunlight. Before she curled up and fell into a deep sleep, she gave herself a thorough cat bath. How she found her way home and what adventures she had along the way we will never know because cats are good at keeping secrets.

Time passed. The grocer found another solution to his mice problem, and Mother continued to be a customer. Herky made a point of staying close to home, rarely venturing further than the neighbor's fishpond. Dad again looked forward to being greeted each evening by his cat. Mother learned a valuable lesson about parenting. At least I know, after we children were born, she never offered to loan us out.

Dänna Wilberg

Dänna Wilberg, a multiple award-winning, short filmmaker, produces and hosts two local television programs in Sacramento, California—Paranormal Connection and Story Connection.

Dänna has authored the Grace Simms romantic suspense trilogy, *The Red Chair*, *The Grey Door*, and *The Black Dress*. Current works in progress include a paranormal suspense series based on  her short film, *Borrowed Time*, featuring intuitive Suzanne Cash.

Visit her website at www.dannawilberg.com.

DÄNNA WILBERG

Not Fair

The young girl pivoted on one gold sneaker, assessing her profile in the full-length mirror. Her uncles called her "Dolly." Aunts, cousins, and so-called friends called her "Jugs," "Tramp," and other demeaning names under their breath and behind her back.

Hand on hip and shoulders squared, she twisted, feet apart. Her ginger mane brushed the base of her spine. A fake giggle escaped her glossy lips. "What do you think?" she asked, batting her eyes. "Too much?" She crinkled her nose and tossed her hair.

Stacy shrugged. "Mama will never let you leave the house like that, June Lee."

Just then, Stacy's mother called from the first floor of their modest bungalow. "You girls ready yet?"

The two girls barreled down the stairs. The flyer taped to the fridge caught June Lee's eye, and she broke out in a classic movie song. "Our state fair is a great state fair. Don't miss it. Don't even be late!"

"June Lee Jillian Moore, don't think you are wearing those itty-bitty shorts to the fair." Her aunt dipped one hand into a brown grocery bag. She pulled out a large can of pork and beans, set it down, and fetched another. "Scantily dressed females invite trouble."

"Aunt Sue, everyone wears short-shorts to the fair. It's what American girls do."

"Not *that* short! You're *twelve*, for Pete's sake. It's bad enough you have those." She paused, choosing her words carefully. "You're too young for boys to be devouring you with their eyes."

"We're almost thirteen," Stacy piped in. Born only two days after June Lee, Stacy remained six inches shorter and flat as a board.

"Don't be in such a hurry to grow up," Stacy's mom said, redirecting her command to her niece. "Go put some *clothes* on. Once I get these things put away, we can leave."

"But you said I could ride with June Lee!"

"June Lee is riding with *us*."

Stacy stomped away. June Lee followed in her tiny shadow, muttering, "I'm lucky I can even go! Your mom told my mom we were cookin' somethin' up!"

"Did you bring mascara?" asked Stacy. Her china-blue eyes followed her cousin's hand to the back pocket of her skimpy shorts. June Lee pulled the small cylinder half way out, revealing the Maybelline logo. "Rad," Stacy said.

June Lee pouted. "Do *you* think I look like a hooker?"

"Not exactly. Don't hookers get paid?"

"You're no help!" June Lee threw herself on the bed.

Stacy rummaged through her closet. "Here, wear these," she said, tossing her moaning counterpart a pair of turquoise capris.

"Now I don't *match*."

"That top does nothing for those jugs of yours anyway. Here, this one," she said, holding the fabric up to the light. "Like Mama says, the more left to the imagination, the better. Besides, June Lee, we can't both wear shorts; we'd look like twins!"

"I'd rather wear pants anyways," said June Lee. Those metal seats get mighty hot. Darn near scorched my butt last year." She wiggled into the capris and a white, sleeveless blouse with lace trim. The thin fabric stretched across her chest. The buttons strained against the overflow. "I look like a freak."

"Bobby Johnson's gonna hyperventilate when he sees you."

"Bobby Johnson is a senior. He's not interested in me."

"Wanna bet?"

***

July's sun scorched the fairgrounds, the asphalt soft beneath sneakers. "Meet me by the bottle toss at two o'clock to check in," said Stacy's mom, handing each girl a five-dollar bill. "Get yourself lunch and some ride tickets." Finger-lifting her daughter's dimpled chin, she added, "You'll get the rest when you check in at two." To June Lee, she issued one last warning: "Behave yourself. I see the heads you're turning already. Those aren't boys; they're scumbags. I promised your mother I'd keep an eye on you. Bottle toss. Two o'clock. Promise?"

June Lee's jaw tightened. Stacy resorted to eye rolling, but both girls promised and went to stand in line at the ticket booth. The temperature had risen to triple digits. Scents of greasy corn dogs and cotton candy mingled with sweat, cloying perfumes, and aftershave. As the girls snaked the aisles, men zeroed in on June Lee's assets, sneaking a peek when their wives or girlfriends weren't looking. One man didn't disguise his lust and offered to take the girls to have some *real* fun. When the girls declined, he broke out in a deep-throated cackle, claiming they didn't know what they were missing.

Gold tennis shoes gleamed against the blue sky. The girls shrieked as the Ferris wheel stopped at the top. They rocked the bucket seat and stamped their feet. They bellowed Queen's victory song, oblivious to the man in the gondola below who rubbernecked and eye-danced from one tween to the other. What Stacy lacked in the mammary department, she made up with her Kewpie-doll smile and attractive legs. Although Stacy turned a few heads herself, the couple seemed mismatched. Often, Stacy was mistaken for June Lee's little sister.

Back on the flat asphalt, the girls heard hawkers beckon them to try their luck. Tattooed arms waved stuffed Teddy bears in the air. They tempted passersby with cuddly prizes and cunning challenges. Bobby Johnson leaned against a makeshift castle at the end of the row.

"Hey, June Bug. Break a balloon and win a prize." His eyes dripped down her body like hot fudge on a sundae. "Give ya an extra try for a buck." He leaned forward until his breath tickled her ear. "Show me *your* balloons; I'll give you any prize you want."

Stacy giggled. "Toldja."

June Lee socked Stacy's arm. "Shut up." She turned back to Bobby and said, "No thanks. Toys are for kids."

Bobby squinted against the sun. "That's right. Heard you're gonna be thirteen in a few days. What was I thinkin'?" He smoothed his hands down the front of his Levi's, hooking his thumbs in his pockets. He thrust his pelvis forward. "Well now, I can think of a better prize. Girls tell me I have quite the gift." He moved closer, pressing his prize against her hip.

June Lee's heart drummed in her ears. The temperature seemed to rise ten degrees. Perspiration trickled down her temples and the back of her neck. Fringed bangs stuck to her forehead. Her aunt's words buzzed in her head: *Men are born to fish. First they bait the hook with their sweet-talk and shiny baubles, and then they reel you in, nice and slow.* June Lee's amber eyes blazed into Bobby's baby blues. "You're a pig, Bobby Johnson. A dirty-minded pig!" June Lee grabbed Stacy's arm and yanked her away from the booth. Bobby's face turned crimson. He threatened to beat the snot out of her.

June Lee beelined for the tarmac.

Stacy stumbled behind. "Why'd you do that?"

"Do what? Cut his line?"

"What'd he say?" Stacy asked.

"Never mind. Let's go get some lemonade and meet up with your mom."

By eight 'clock that evening, the Ferris wheel stood sentinel against the sun's soft corona. Stars glittered above; lights sparkled below. The stroller brigade thinned out. Leather and lace prevailed. From the center of the tarmac, music chattered from three different directions—blues, country, and rock. The girls chose country.

Twenty deep from the stage, young hips began to sway, keeping time with the beat. Stacy's face scrunched. A high note broke free from her lips. Her fist shot into the air. June Lee bounced on her heels as music penetrated their souls. Stacy noticed a man step behind her cousin. He stepped close, his body touching hers. June Lee stepped forward. Stacy stayed put. After all, they were immersed in a crowd of fair-goin', beer-drinkin', music-lovin' crazies. Everyone was hootin', hollerin', and having a good time, right? Stacy watched her cousin step to her right. The man bumped her again, and June Lee stepped left. Stacy sang at the top of her lungs, ignoring the man encroaching on their territory until June Lee shouted, "Come on. Let's go!" Stacy pretended not to hear and sang the next verse with the band. June Lee yanked her arm. Stacy pulled away. The man moved closer.

By the time Stacy turned around, her cousin was being swallowed up in the shifting crowd. Stacy moved towards her, but it was too late. June Lee was out of sight. "Dammit," Stacy cursed out loud. She maneuvered against the flow, nudging people out of her way. She stood on tiptoes, ducked under flailing arms, barged between couples two-stepping in place. No June Lee. She fought her way to the edge of the crowd, glancing behind her, calling June Lee's name. An older woman shoved her and yelled, "Get a "grip." Stacy threatened to grip her neck and squeeze. She knew her mother would be mad if she found out they got separated. However, she wouldn't catch the blame. Her mom and Aunt Sue would most likely accuse June Lee of "whoring around" or something equally trite, like "showing off those damn jugs." Stacy tried not to panic, but her veins filled with ice. She had a bad feeling about the man who came out of nowhere. *Why did she pull away?*

Dark now, Stacy shuffled toward the tarmac with a thousand other people, all-the-while searching for June Lee. They had begged to be let out on their own and, crossed their hearts to stay glued at the hip. Stacy's own words haunted her: "We're almost thirteen!"

***

Stacy crumpled the flyer in her hand and tossed it into the trash. "C'mon, Mom!" her oldest protested, egged on by her smidge of a friend. "Why can't we go to the fair? Jenn's mom said she'd drive!"

"Not a safe place for young girls."

"But we're almost thirteen!"

Stacy studied the daughter who had blossomed into a spittin' image of June Lee, the cousin no one seemed to miss. As if cruelly fated, Stacy watched her daughter, like June Lee, bear the brunt of jokes and jealousy from family and friends. Her heart broke again and again, remembering the last time she saw her cousin and the look of desperation in June Lee's eyes when she grabbed her arm. Stacy held onto the guilt. . .*if only I hadn't pulled away.*

Jill K. Yaranon

J ill K. (Katie) Yaranon is living the dream on her horse ranch in Cool, California. She is president of the local horse club, Divide Horsemen's Association, which advocates for equestrian trails in the communities of Cool, Georgetown, Pilot Hill, and surrounding hamlets (yes, there really is a town named Cool). She has three exceptional trail horses that faithfully carry her over the rugged trails and the many challenges they present—like  swift water crossings, rattlesnakes, wild turkeys, but only the occasional drug lord.

JILL K. YARANON
Lost in the Pink

Every summer, in the spirit of adventure, I make it a point to get out of my comfort zone and ride some new trails. So when my riding buddy Jane invited me to ride in Georgetown with her, I jumped at the chance. We trailered our trusty horses up to the Balderson staging area above the town of Georgetown for a short and easy ride through the pine forests. Since Jane lives up in this neck of the woods, she was familiar with the trails—or so she thought. I guess it would depend on your definition of familiar. Familiar as in "I know the way blindfolded" or familiar as in "I might be able to find the right trail if I am very, very lucky and the trails are marked with lovely signage reading 'This Way Back to Wentworth Springs Road' or 'Turn here for Civilization'." Unfortunately for us apparently the exact definition of familiar was not Jane's strong suit even though she studied the trailhead map for at least five minutes before we mounted.

"Look, Katie, I think we should take this short loop here -- then we'll wind up back here at the parking lot in about an hour and a half and go get a sandwich and a Coke at the deli in Georgetown. Won't that be fun?"

I could see right away that this was my kind of ride, and, in fact, I was already planning whether to have jalapeno cheese or provolone on my sandwich. So really why bother looking at the map? Jane had it under control. Besides I didn't have my glasses with me and from what I could tell the map looked pretty much like every other trailhead map. Lots of lines and tracks that all seemed to end up back at the staging area-eventually.

It all started so perfectly. The trail was wide and shady--lined with towering green pines that shielded us from the hot midday sun. We rode along the main trail happily chatting for the first hour until we came to a split. One side was marked with fluttering pink ribbons and the other side dark, morose, now beginning to get annoying, green pine trees.

"I think we should follow the pink ribbons," Jane suggests breezily waving her hand in the vague direction of the ribbon-be-decked trail.

"Why?" I want to know. Is there any good reason to merrily follow pink ribbons just because they gaily festoon the trees? I mean what about the map back at the trailhead?

"Let's just take the loop that you know—the one we saw back at the trailhead," I say.

"What loop on the map?"

A little red flag begins to wave in the back of my brain. Or maybe it's a little pink flag.

But I follow Jane's lead, and we head down the pink ribbon marked trail certain that I am a neurotic worrywart.

After another forty-five minutes of riding, we are deep in the forest, and I am going to scream if I see another pink ribbon tied to tree branches. They are tied everywhere--tied on high branch-es, tied on low branches, dangling on the right, fluttering on the left. "Whoever marked this trail was on drugs" I mumble to Jane's back. Now we notice some have black polka dots, some have wavy blue lines, and some are unadorned in their sinister bubblegum innocence. Jane rides in front leading the way, and she has become curiously silent.

"Jane this doesn't look right. Maybe we should double back."

"You mean go back the way we came?" She turns around and looks at me with a vacant stare.

Uh-oh. The red flag is waving full force now, and there is a warning bell ringing too.

"Jane do you recognize this part of the trail? Are we going the right way? Do you know where we are?"

Her face is pale, and she is sweating profusely.

"I don't feel so good. I don't think I can ride anymore."

Oh, no problem. We'll just call a taxi to swing by and get you.

So there we are surrounded by the damn ubiquitous pink ribbons, Jane is barfing in the bushes, and I am completely clueless how to get back to the staging area. And did I mention that now it's close to a hundred degrees outside, and I am out of water?

After hurling up her guts, Jane is resting on a stump, and we hear the rumble of a motor in the distance. A gray truck pops onto the trail through the dust cloud. Jane stands up, and I move our horses to the side of the single lane track. The teenage driver is frantically waving to us out his driver's window as he bumps along the road towards us and stops.

"Do you know where Pig Hollow Road is? I have to deliver a package there, and it's not on any map I have." He looks past us down the dark, pine-studded trail like he has suddenly landed on Mars.

"I think we passed it somewhere back that way, right after we turned off the paved road," I wave my hand in the general direction we just rode from.

I can't imagine what necessity someone would need to have delivered to Pig Hollow Road-- not to mention someone crazy enough to deliver it. The trails we've been riding are deeply rutted, unpaved, and there have been no signs of human habitation for miles. I look into the truck bed for the critical necessity that someone would have to go to Herculean efforts to deliver out here. Possibly a part to fix a broken down tractor stuck in a field, a lifesaving diabetes medicine, a subpoena maybe...

"Forget Pig Hollow, we have no idea where it is. There haven't been signs for miles. Ask him if he has any water," Jane's weak voice croaks from somewhere in the bushes.

"Oh, for Pete's sake Jane, please tell me you did not drink the last of your water?"

Apparently Jane is still strong enough to give me the finger. She is very cranky when she is nauseous.

The delivery kid is also out of liquids too. He shakes his head mournfully and holds up an empty liter water bottle.

"I got nothin'. I was hoping you had some water," he says as he wipes the sweat off his brow with a towel. He puts the truck in gear and chugs by in a puff of dust only to turn around at the next clearing and head back from where he came. I clearly hear him mumbling as he rolls by--- something about "Crazy ass people living in BFE", before disappearing into a dusty brownish haze. For those of you not familiar with BFE, we are about as close to it as you can get without actually traveling to the Middle East. And the poor delivery kid can't get away fast enough.

Even so, my partner has parting advice for the hapless delivery kid.

"Whatever you do, don't follow the damn pink ribbons," she screams wildly as he careens down the road.

Between Jane's bouts of nausea and my hysterical rantings about fiends who come out and mark the trail with pink ribbons in the dead of night, we follow the truck's trail of dust hoping the kid can find his way back to civilization. On each side of the trial there are small offshoot trails that are marked with the devilish pink ribbons-- there is no way to tell which trail returns to the staging area. So we plod along in the suffocating heat. Jane is not able to ride for more than a few minutes at a time, and walking makes her dizzy. The horses are wet with sweat, and none of us had any water for hours. We have not crossed a creek, stream or trickle of water. How in the world can these trees stay so green? Around every turn, we expect to see something we recognize-a sign post, a fence, a mailbox, even a big rock would be something different then pine trees. Finally, like a lake in the middle of the desert, we see a main road straight ahead. Well, "main road" is loosely defined here. Let's just say it is a paved road. Jane is ready to weep with relief.

"Flag down the first car you see," she groans gripping her stomach

"What if it's an axe murderer ready to go on a rampage?" I say. I think it's important we consider our odds. Death by dehydration or death by an axe murderer.

"I don't care who it is or what they look like. I'm so sick I'd go with an escaped felon if he had water and an aspirin," Jane yells.

"Don't get your hopes up," I yell back. "I'm not stopping him if he looks scary."

Jane hisses at me "I don't care if he is a drug crazed inbred Neanderthal man. I've got to have water and get my meds from the truck."

Jane really does look terrible, and so I bravely walk to the middle of the road prepared to flag down a toothless, wild-eyed mountain man with an ax resting snugly across his lap. Jane, I might add, is safely throwing up in the bushes--definitely hidden from view in case of a violent and bloody attack. The vehicle crests the hill, and a brown delivery truck appears.

"Hallelujah, Jane-- it's a UPS truck!" I jump up and down and wave my hands just in case the driver could miss a woman and her two horses standing in the middle of the deserted road.

"Stop him!" she screams. "Ask him to help us."

By now I have got to admit that we may be too far out to ride back even if we were sure of the trail. And five hours of pine tree therapy is enough for anyone.

So I stand my ground in the middle of the road, wave my arms like I'm at the Macy's day Thanksgiving Parade and try not to look like a hysterical, bedraggled, hopelessly lost PMS woman popping out of the woods where quite likely no human has ever been seen before. Even in my desperation, I guess I don't look too bizarre, because the driver stops, leans his head out the door and smiles at me.

"You all right?"

"No, we need help," wails Jane from the bushes. "I'm really sick, and I need my medication. Can you take me back to Balderston staging area? Do you know where it is from here?" He looks at Jane peering out from behind a tree.

"I know exactly where it is. This is my regular route." There are angels even on UPS routes.

And so Jane, surprisingly spry for a woman on her death bed, sprints over to the UPS truck and hops into the little extra seat the driver pulls down.

"You ladies are about eight miles away. I have to deliver this one more package and then I will take you over there." Apparently package delivery is big out here in the trees. What could he possibly be delivering? There is no human life for miles. But the last thing I want to do is delay him or piss him off and have him drive away from two weary women wandering around in the woods.

"You wait here with the horses, and I'll come back with the rig to get you," Jane says as she settles herself on the jump seat. I hold the horses and watch the big brown truck go over the mountain and drop out of sight.

So for me, things don't improve much. I mean I am still out of water. I have not had my sandwich. I have no clue where I am, and now I have two tuckered out horses besides. I sit down on a big stump to think and let the horses graze the sparse grass. Mainly I think back on our trail ride just to make sure I didn't say anything offensive to Jane that would get her mad at me. I mean if I knew my life depended on Jane…As it starts to get dark in the deep shade forest, my stomach growls and rumbles and I feel a little light headed. The forest is silent. There is no bird song, no voices, no distant thrum of traffic--just me and my thoughts. Maybe Jane is as hungry as I am and she felt like she had to go to the deli without me? Maybe once she took her medication she slipped into a delusional state and forgot she was even riding with me. If she does remember our predicament, will she remember where she left me? Maybe the UPS has relaxed their hiring standards, and the driver really was a deranged psychotic rapist… As the sun slips behind the mountain and turns the trees into black paper cutouts, I hear the drone of a vehicle and rattle of my trailer coming up the road. Hooray! She remembered us!

She roars over the crest of the hill and toots the horn.

"Need a ride, Sweetie?" She grins at me from the cab. Her color is good, and she is positively beaming with good health. What kind of meds did she have in the truck anyway? We water the horses and let them drink their fill before loading them. As we drive towards town, the pink ribbons become a distant memory, and I am satisfied with another day to be alive and a big fat juicy roast beef sandwich when we finally get to Wharton's deli. Which, I might add, Jane pays for!

Matthias Mendezona

Matthias Mendezona is the author of *How Sweet the Mango, No? The Journey of a Hispanic Amerasian,* a story that depicts the universal struggles of a man, his land, conflicting identities, and true heritage.

Matthias was born to a Basque father and a Filipino-American mother in the island of Mindanao, Philippines. Jesuit-educated, he grew up on a coconut farm with a jungle at the back of the  house and the beach up front, spending much of his childhood summers with his American grandfather who taught him about the tropical jungle, wildlife, and interacting with the ethnic tribe called the Subano.

He is also the author of *Rumination: Of Steeping and Loss, then New Life,* an award-winning book of poetry, lavishly illustrated, from which he has excerpted the poem "Woodpeckers at Dry Creek."

MATTHIAS MENDEZONA

Woodpeckers at Dry Creek

The woodpeckers are back.
What warm place do they find in winter?
Savannah? Louisiana? Honduras?
It matters not, for it is March and they are back in Roseville.

"Ratatat!" I hear one's beak against a tree.
"Ratatat!" Replies another in the distance.
I walk through the trees in my usual way.
"I wish you no harm, just passing through.
I wish you peace." I speak to the trees
like my mountain tribe friends taught me
as a child.

I hear again the woodpeckers.
Red and black they are,
smaller by far than their Asian brothers.
And their Asian brothers flash briefly before me,
as a young man peers through forest vines
in wonder
at a large bird red and white

pecking rapidly on a tree
with a crown too tall to see.
The rainforest and birds of then
vanish from memory, and I hear yet again
the Roseville woodpeckers of now.

"I wish you no harm….." I say, and move on.

William J. Blaylock

Bill Blaylock is a United States Army veteran. He has post-traumatic stress disorder, but he only discovered it some forty years after his service in Vietnam.

His story—nearly forty different jobs, isolation, flashbacks, anger, and insomnia—are chronicled in his book *Invisible: PTSD's Stealth Attack on a Vietnam War Veteran.*

Finding almost by accident that writing his story was therapeutic, he has since gone on to establish a writing support group in El Dorado County California for other veterans suffering with PTSD.

His fictional short story, "Forged for War," actually has ties to the story in his book *Invisible*, and Leonard is a real person who served with Bill in Vietnam.

WILLIAM J. BLAYLOCK
Forged for War

My family history began in the Commonwealth of Pennsylvania, April 29, 1897, though my father was born in 1920 and grew up around iron works and steel manufacturers in the Commonwealth area. WWII started in January of 1942, and on December 9, 1942, he entered the into the Marine Corps.

Through his military career, he and his family members were involved in all branches of service. During his career, he did both good and bad, and he prayed that the good outweighed the bad! He was not a commissioned officer though he did work closely with them.

This is where his story begins. He was young, almost twenty-three years, and a new and proud Marine. He had completed Marine Corps Recruit Training, also known as boot camp and then further training at the Infantry Training Battalion, both at Camp Pendleton, California. The Second World War was in full swing with almost every nation involved.

After a short leave, probably intended for him to say his final goodbyes in early March 1943, he was sent to the Pacific Island of Guam. His war experience started soon after arriving. While on guard duty his second night, his partner and he caught two enemy soldiers trying to crawl under the barbed wire.

His partner yelled, "Halt!" One of them froze in place, but the other lunged toward him. In what seemed only a split second, he had stabbed him in his chest and slit his throat. As soon as his body hit the ground, the first soldier charged. Dad threw himself at him in response to his attack, stabbing him in his rib section before his partner and fellow Marines arrived and removed him from his attacker and took the enemy soldier to the corpsman for treatment and later questioning.

That was the first time Dad had killed a men, let alone seen a dead body. That was his first taste of blood, and, unfortunately, there would be many, many more. But he was sent there to do what ever was necessary to help and save his fellow Marines in their service to "God, Mother, and Country, and the Corps."

After that first experience with the violence of death, Dad was assigned to assist and tag along with a corpsman. At first he thought it was going to be a easy, time-wasting assignment. Man, was he wrong about that. He was still around a lot of blood, the blood of his fellow Americans. It hurt him to see them suffering and in so much pain. He was able to help in ways he hadn't thought about before. Sometimes I did good things, simple things. For example, corpsman Bob and he would spend hours cutting gauze and making bandages so that they would be ready when he needed them. A few times he had to help make an emergency amputation in the field of combat. He didn't like cutting his own guys, but it was the only way he could save them. It took him a while to overcome his sadness and depression about that. Sometimes in his anger and frustration, he would throw himself against the wall, and just stay there for a while, trying to figure out the madness of this thing called war. After a while, he accepted the fact that he had actually done good things, and he started to appreciate himself and my strengths.

Dad finished out the rest of the war mostly in the Pacific but did get to Europe just before the war ended, though he didn't see much action there. He did end up going to one of Germany's many concentration camps. That was the worst, most shocking, humiliating, humbling, and sorrowful experiences of his entire being. The Nazis didn't just confine and torture Jewish people; they had people of all races, religions, and backgrounds. For many years after the war, it still made him sick to think about it. The narcissistic Nazi regime had a twisted, evil ideology, based on malice toward the Jewish religion and people. What a waste.

After the war, Dad had a few years of relative peace, and it was during that time frame that I was conceived. There was still fighting occasionally, but America didn't declare war on anyone. Dad did some time at Camp Pendleton as a drill instructor. He said that it was fun, messing with the recruits. He would scare them with his razor-sharp edge, then threaten to chew them up and spit them out with his jagged, rigid, back side. What fun he had!

Here we go again, no declaration of war, just a conflict. August 2, 1950, Dad was in the shore assault at Pusan, Korea. He, or rather the Fifth Marine Regiment, Third Marine Division first made contact with the enemy on August 7 at Chindong-ni, roughly fifty miles west of Pusan. Over the next twelve days, they pushed back the North Koreans to establish and stabilize a perimeter for the defense of the Pusan. They were not without loss of life, but it was small compared to the heavy losses taken by the North Koreans in that first engagement. The rest of the war went back and forth with us pushing them, and them pushing back. The Marines lost a lot of lives, but they also had attrition from the brutal effects of frostbite, mostly with the loss of fingers, toes, and other extremities.

Damn, that was a miserable war. Dad said that he had never felt so cold. Liquid would freeze on that same sharp edge he used to scare the recruits. Dad's older brothers' two sons and a nephew were enlisted in the Army, Army special forces, and Navy SEALs (back then, they were called "Frogmen"). Again he saw a lot of death and agony and was akin to much of it himself. He said, "It sure was tough to find good things to do."

A truce was agreed upon on July 27, 1953, and dad was sure glad to leave. He spent his next few years shuffling around in a supply depot until his retirement.

In January 1965, I enlisted and was assigned to the Third Marine Division. It was March 8, 1965, when I arrived in Vietnam. We flew in on C-130 Hercules aircraft and landed about ten miles west of Da Nang, where we met up with the Third Battalion, Ninth Marines, who had made a rather lack-luster shore invasion earlier that morning. After storming the beach, they were greeted by photographers and Vietnamese school girls! I was glad that I wasn't in the "Third of the Ninth!"

In my career, I served with a lot of good men and Marines. They took care of me, and I took care of them. Just like my Dad,

I did both good and bad, but always for a just cause.

It was March 8, 1968, when I met Leonard. We were in a ditch, trying to protect ourselves from a rocket and mortar attack on our convoy. When the shelling stopped, we started a conversation. Right away, I liked Leonard. Everyone else called him Len. It was then and there that I actually joined the Army. It wasn't a formal resignation from the Corps and an official swearing-in to the Army. I just started working with and was attached to Leonard. From that day on, I was by Len's side. Through my many years in the Corps, I had acquired scores of deep scars, and understandably had—try as I might—lost my fine edge. Leonard became my closest friend, even above the close bond of combat warriors. Len, with time, was able to smooth away most of my many scars and bring me back to a comfortable, combat ready attitude. I was once again honed to a fighting edge.

When Leonard left "The Nam" to return home, I had to stay because my tour was not yet over. We said our stirring farewells, promising never to forget each other. I went back to the Corps after Leonard left.

It was mid-April of 1971 when I fell. It was during a firefight in the jungle-clad mountains surrounding Khe Sanh, during our second and final abandonment of the forward base. I went down in the deep grass, unable to see up and too deep to be seen by either friend or foe. I kept sinking deeper and deeper into the soft, muddy, red soil. I never left Vietnam.

I was never found, my leather wrapped handle became dry and brittle and broke away from my spine. My steel, saw-tooth-backed frame rusted. Eventually, I became part of the land.

Now you know my story. My name is KA-BAR. I am a Marine utility knife.

Semper Fi.

About NCPA

Northern California Publishers & Authors (NCPA) is an alliance of independent publishers, authors, and associate publishing professionals centered in the Sacramento, California, area.

Its purpose is to foster, encourage, and educate authors, small-press publishers, and others interested in becoming authors and publishers.

The association is home to many award-winning writers, published authors, aspiring writers, and small publishers who are committed to becoming the best force to network, pool knowledge, share resources, educate, monitor the industry, and exploit new publishing and marketing media.

NCPA hosts monthly meetings, online discussion boards, professional development events, and an annual awards contest.

Visit the NCPA web page at www.NorCalPA.org

www.ingramcontent.com/pod-product-compliance
Lightning Source LLC
Chambersburg PA
CBHW051256250626
47155CB00009B/3321